THE REDROCK CHRONICLES

CENTER BOOKS ON SPACE, PLACE, AND TIME

George F. Thompson, Series Founder and Director

Published in cooperation with the Center for American Places
SANTA FE, NEW MEXICO, AND HARRISONBURG, VIRGINIA

THE REDROCK CHRONICLES

Saving Wild Utah

T. H. Watkins

PHOTOGRAPHS BY THE AUTHOR

The Johns Hopkins University Press   Baltimore and London

The Johns Hopkins University Press
2715 North Charles Street
Baltimore, Maryland 21218-4363
www.press.jhu.edu

Portions of this book first appeared in *Wilderness, Audubon, Sierra,* and *National Geographic* magazines, and the author wants to thank the Wilderness Society, the National Audubon Society, the Sierra Club, and the National Geographic Society for permission to reprint them here.

Library of Congress Cataloging-in-Publication data
will be found at the end of this book.

A catalog record for this book is available from the British Library.

ISBN 0-8018-6237-X   ISBN 0-8018-6238-8 (pbk.)

FRONTISPIECE Redrock walls, in the proposed Escalante Canyons Wilderness, in Grand Staircase–Escalante National Monument (1989)

To the memory of **WALLACE STEGNER** (1909–1993).

No writer ever gave the wild country of southern Utah

better form. No writer could ever hope to.

CONTENTS

*I*T *IS A LOVELY AND TERRIBLE wilderness, such a wilderness as Christ and the prophets went out into; harshly and beautifully colored, broken and worn until its bones are exposed, its great sky without a smudge or taint from Technocracy, and in hidden corners and pockets under its cliffs the sudden poetry of springs. Save a piece of country like that intact, and it does not matter in the slightest that only a few people every year will go into it. That is precisely its value.*

WALLACE STEGNER, "Coda: Wilderness Letter,"
The Sound of Mountain Water (1969)

THE REDROCK CHRONICLES

INTRODUCTION: HOME OF MY HEART

I AM HELPLESSLY ADDICTED to this place, this wondrous geographic puzzle of canyons turning in on themselves, of upthrust plateaus and big blisterlike mountains, of multicolored rocks all layered and bent and broken, of curling rivers dammed by beavers and shaded by grandfather cottonwoods, of horizon-wide sweeps of sunlit emptiness and gracile unknown places where darkness hides and will not tell its name.

While flying cross-country from Washington, D.C., to Los Angeles, as I used to do more often than I care to think about, I usually began to fidget with anticipation whenever our route took us near the point at which New Mexico, Colorado, Utah, and Arizona meet—the Four Corners. I would have been waiting for this confluence for much of the trip, and, when finding myself on the wrong side of the plane, was entirely capable of getting out of my seat at the right moment to lean over some hapless fellow passenger in order to look out through a murky square of Plexiglas to see whatever I could see of southern Utah. Not much, usually, but once in a while, when the angle of our flight path was just right, I would want to grab other passengers and shout, *There! Right down there! The Abajos! The Kaiparowits Plateau!* Or even, on especially wondrous occasions, *The Escalante! Look! Look! Isn't that great?* You'd think that was my own home I was looking down on from the empyrean height of thirty-seven thousand feet. Sometimes I think it was—and still is.

On the face of it, this seems unlikely. I was born, surrounded by orange groves, in the San Bernardino Valley of southern California. When I reached the age of reason (twenty-four, in my case), I moved to the San Francisco Bay area, where I lived for sixteen years. Then it was to Manhattan for six years, and after that to Washington, D.C., where I resided for more than fifteen years before moving to Montana to teach. For the most part, I was a perfectly adjusted urban animal. True, my wife was held up at knifepoint in the foyer of our New York City apartment once, and I was held up twice—once at gunpoint on a dark North Beach street in San Francisco, once at knifepoint in the foyer of our apartment in residential Washington. In none of our three cities were we ever unaware of the perils as well as the amenities of city life. Still, the trade-off seemed reasonable somehow, though that may just have been a kind of urban denial.

At any rate, what did I need with southern Utah, of all places? Why do I still get the twitches and the clammydamps if I am away from it for too long? Why do I go back two and sometimes three times a year? Why do I yearn to vanish within one of its canyons for days on end—and sometimes do? Why do I keep writing about it and bending my puny efforts in its defense? Why does it speak to me with such power when I have known this country for less than fifteen years?

What I have instead of answers are memories. Here is my first: In the fall of 1986, the Governing Council of the Wilderness Society held its annual meeting in Springdale, Utah, the "gateway" community to Zion National Park. When all the bureaucratic bushwa was done, both society staff and council members were encouraged, as always, to experience some of the country they had come together to talk about protecting. I took a drive though Zion and was suitably impressed by the enormous stone monoliths that have made it famous. Impressed—not transformed.

But one day a bunch of us took a hike. We were driven by van out of the park and down to a little Arizona town named Colorado City just south of the Utah-Arizona border. The town was once named Short Creek, but after a group of its Mormon citizens had been rounded up and arrested for practicing polygamy in 1953 (I can still remember the newsreel coverage of this event), it had changed its name. Its name, maybe, but not all of its habits. The town was full of uncommonly big houses. From the front doors of many of these houses, women in long skirts watched us drive by. Behind most of the women could be seen small children. There were a lot of rooms in the houses, and a lot of somber-faced children seemed to be peeking around the skirts of a lot of somber-faced women; I was not surprised to learn later that many Colorado City families still practice polygamy, in spite of the fact that it remains illegal and that the Church of Jesus Christ of Latter-day Saints itself officially banned the practice a century ago.

That brief interlude in Colorado City gave me a frisson of connection to a past I had only read about, a time when the history of this region was being written by multi-wived and many-childrened bands of pious and extraordinarily determined settlers sent into the hinterland by Brigham Young to increase and prosper, building little enclaves of Deseret's Mormon empire. But there was something uncannily familiar about the scene, too. My hometown of San Bernardino had once been a similar enclave of Mormonhood, and while it had grown far beyond those beginnings by the time I was born, there still were plenty of LDS folk around. I could remember my best friend's mother standing in the kitchen, tall and unsmiling in her gray floor-length skirt and her dull white blouse buttoned to the neck, long blonde-gray hair pulled back into an unrelenting bun, not a shadow of makeup to be found on her face. She could have been any one of the mothers I saw that afternoon in Colorado City. My friend could have been any one of the children. (So far as I know, however, my friend's mother was the only wife involved in that particular family.)

A couple of young Mormon men who had been hired as guides met us at a service station in Colorado City, then led us back up into Utah to the mouth of a place called Water Canyon, one of the Bureau of Land Management's best-kept secrets. We all piled out of the vans, got our daypacks and box lunches together, and started hiking up the little canyon along a narrow creek whose banks were thick with Mormon tea, desert willows, clumps of mountain sage, and stands of ancient cottonwoods. The leaves of the cottonwoods were just beginning to turn, and we marched for a time beneath a canopy of green and gold through which the sun sent blades of light stabbing into the sandy, leaf-littered trail.

The higher we climbed up the bed of the chattering creek that had made the place, the more narrow the canyon became, red rock walls closing in on both sides, opening up every now and then into elegant little alcoves of beautifully sculptured stone swirled with maroon and ivory bands, the creek's tan-and-white banks as smooth and unmarked as a Caribbean beach at dawn, ferns clustered in dark wet corners, trickles of water and bright green beards of moss ornamenting the slickrock faces. All this was cool and lovely and inviting, but nothing unexpected, nothing I had not seen in photographs. Then we neared the top of the canyon and entered a thick grove of mountain maple whose sunlit leaves fluttered and tossed in the breeze coming down off the plateau above us. Up here, the leaves had fully turned. Their color was unlike anything I had ever seen, a thin, nearly translucent purple, and there seemed to be millions of them swarming around our heads and shoulders like thick clouds of lavender butterflies. With the others in our group, I found myself raising my arms and turning in a circle, laughing in simple pleasure at so much unexpected beauty.

Was this an epiphany? Maybe. What I know with certainty is that, ever since that luminous moment on the side of a little canyon somewhere north of Colorado City, I have spent as much time as I can in this southern Utah landscape, driving its roads, flying over it, hiking into its canyons, camping along its rivers, soaking it up, taking it in, sometimes writing about it, most of the time just thinking about its warps and tangles of rock and sky. My own photographs of the place adorn the wall of my office in Bozeman, where I can see them at all times. Southern Utah has become the standard against which I measure the character and quality of natural beauty everywhere. I can love other country. I can love the long sweet curves of the big Missouri as it slides through the grasslands of eastern Montana, or the rocky, surf-beaten coves of the northern California coast, the misty old mountains of the southern Appalachians, the Joshua Tree forests on Cima Dome in the California desert, the rolling tundra of the coastal plain of Arctic Refuge in Alaska, the Bitterroots and the Bighorns. I can love these wonderful places that I have known to one degree or another, but in none do I feel so fully alive in my own skin as I do here in the place I have called the home of my heart.

So. Be it known to all those present that what follows is not so much a text as a celebration. I will give you history here, both of the land and of the people who have made a sojourning in it; I will describe what I have learned of the land's geology, of its sights and colors and smells and sounds; I will tell you something of the demographics of the society the land nurtures today and of what its future might be; and I will rise up on my hind legs and protest in no uncertain terms the corruption that has been done and could still be done to the land, and will offer with all due passion the legislative device of wilderness designation as the necessary means of saving it.

But, above all, and I make no apologies for it, what I will give you here is an undiluted testament of love.

8

PART ONE: THE PLACE

MOST OF US HAVE SEEN the photographs of what the astronauts saw when they looked toward home while standing on the moon: a vulnerable blue sphere floating in the unspeakable black enormity of space, its continents faint brown shadows beneath white smears of ocean-born storms like the whorls in a boy's marble, everything else water, water, water, the elixir that marries with the sun's energy to give us all life. Looking at those serene and lovely images, it is hard to remember just how complex and violent the earth is.

I am not talking here about whatever it is human beings may be doing to one another or to the earth at any given moment, much of which is likely to be reprehensible. I am talking about the planet's own complicated morphology. There is nothing serene about it. As a collection of geological and climatic phenomena, the earth is a scarred, bent, cracked, and agitated wreck of a place. Twenty or twenty-five miles below where we stand, magmas bubble up against the thin crust of oceanic and continental plates, all that stands between us and ultimate meltdown, while the plates themselves float over the hot semiliquid sea of the earth's mantle, grinding against one another, crashing into one another, sliding over one another, rattling our bones and our cities with earthquakes, raising up tsunamis to ravage our coastlines, giving birth to the eruption of volcanoes, lava flows oozing out of cracks and incinerating every living thing in their paths, mountains blowing their tops off and spewing ashes across hundreds of square miles like the last rites in some gargantuan funeral ritual. And everywhere, while we watch, erosion relentlessly bleeds away every particle of mountain, plain, and prairie that water can carry to the waiting seas.

If you find all of this hard to believe, just spend some time in the wildlands of southern Utah, where the story is written everywhere you turn. These lands lie at the heart of the Colorado Plateau, 135,000 square miles of uplifted rock (the equivalent space of Ohio, Indiana, and Michigan combined) sitting like a huge island in the earthly continental sea, surrounded on almost all sides by the remnants of once-active volcanoes. The plateau is not one single slab, of course; it is a veritable puzzle of rocks still being fitted together as the earth below and around it continues its relentless saraband, moving things about, shoving things up, tearing things down—a geological Rubik's Cube for scientists who are still sorting things out and probably will be doing so until the candle of our own era has guttered out.

Begin with some of the oldest rocks there are, or at least some of the oldest that can be seen in plateau country. In the depths of the Grand Canyon in the southwestern end of the plateau, and especially in Black Canyon of the Gunnison River on the plateau's easternmost edge, can be found metamorphic schists that date back two billion years, to the middle of the Precambrian era, rocks so old that they were around when the original continent of Pangaea began breaking apart like polar ice in a summer thaw, enormous floes of crust roaming over the globe to become the continental masses of today. Whole mountain ranges have been thrust up or folded, then torn down, then thrust up and folded again since these rocks were born; whole generations of volcanoes have swelled and exploded; whole inland seas have come and gone, while life has evolved from single-celled swimmers hardly bigger than the molecules that made them to whales the size of submarines.

These Archaic rocks, folded and tilted by tectonic collisions and separations and by magmatic pressure from below, then worn flat at their tops by erosion to create an enormous horizontal plain, provided the foundation on which the plateau began to be constructed during the Paleozoic era, beginning with the Cambrian period about 570 million years ago and continuing through much of the Tertiary period of the Cenozoic era, which ended about two million years ago. During the Paleozoic era, the plain rose and fell in elevation as tectonic forces continued the work of continent shaping. Each time the land sank far enough, the sea rushed in to cover it; each time the land slowly rose again, the sea receded, after everything it carried had slowly settled to the bottom to add layer after layer that time and pressure transformed into identifiable laminations of stone, each layer with its own history, its own amalgam of chemicals and other geological spices to give it color and character, together with the fossilized remains of oolites and related forms of algae, as well as ferns, brachiopods, mollusks, crinoids, sea urchins, fishes, aquatic snails, insects, amphibians, dinosaurs, prehistoric mammals, and many other long-vanished players on the evolutionary stage.

During the Mesozoic era, which began about 245 million years ago, the land began to rise again, until, by the beginning of the Cenozoic era 180 million years later, the last of the Paleozoic seas had drained away. In the interim, tectonic forces had begun shoving the Pacific Plate under the North American Plate, an event called the Laramide Orogeny. The pressures from this gargantuan collision created the

Rocky Mountains and the Uinta Upflift, both higher than the Colorado Plateau, while related pressures within the plateau itself produced various uplifts—particularly the San Rafael Swell, the Circle Cliffs Uplift, and the Monument Uplift. During the periods between the invading seas, erosion from each of these uplifts had added alluvial fans and deltas to the mix of seaborne sediments that had come before.

Finally, during the Oligocene epoch, which lasted from about 38 million years ago to about 24 million years ago, most of the still-rising plateau was subjected to millions of years of periodic violence. Earthquakes fractured the layered stone with faults; crustal squeezing folded it; subsidence collapsed chunks of it into old salt domes; internal pressures tilted it up or down or shoved one sedimental layer over another to create long, clifflike monoclines. Volcanism oozed out lava flows and hurled volcanic rock and ash into the evolving landscape, while magma pushed up into new-born faults and, when it could not burst through the crust, created huge bulges called laccoliths, among which Navajo Mountain and the La Sal and Abajo ranges are impressive representatives.

While sedimentation and upheaval had crudely shaped the plateau country, the more painstaking force of erosion gave the land most of the intricate sculpturing we see today. Some of this erosional shaping was the result of wind-driven sand or fracturing during frost heaves or great fluctuations in temperature, but most of it was the work of moving water—rainfall collecting in rivulets, rivulets lacing together to become creeks, then streams, then rivers.

The river of rivers here, of course, was the Colorado. Rising in the Rocky Mountains of Wyoming, the Colorado began meandering across the ancient plateau surface sometime in the late Tertiary era, perhaps 12 million years ago. As it moved, it slowly gathered its main plateau tributaries to it—the Green, the Gunnison, the Dolores, the White, the San Rafael, the Dirty Devil, the Escalante, the San Juan, the Virgin, and the Paria—each of these rivers possessing its own system of tributaries and all of this wondrous flowing, from rain to river, devoted to the eternal task of carrying the plateau to the sea, bit by minuscule bit.

Pounding seasonal rains washed billions of tons of loose topsoil into the rivers, leaving behind isolated spires, goblin-shaped rock sculptures, flat-topped buttes, exposed stone reefs, and mesas, some of them sitting in the middle of wide, plainlike valleys. Riverborne soils joined with tumbling rocks and pebbles and particles of sand to convert the Colorado and its tributaries into great cutting machines that ate their way into the ever-rising plateau so swiftly that they were able to retain their old meandering patterns while knifing intricate canyon systems hundreds and then thousands of feet deep—Labyrinth, Zion, Glen, Cataract, Desolation, Black Canyon of the Gunnison, the canyons of the Dirty Devil, the canyons of the Escalante, and the deepest and most awesome of them all, the Grand Canyon—each of them revealing, in one exposed layer after the other, all the history that the land embodied.

Down and down the rivers sliced, through the grays of conglomerates and shales and volcanic breccias, through pink and purple and blood-red limestones, each particular layer the child of millions of years of sedimentation, compression, and erosion. But mostly the rivers cut through sandstone, generation after generation of sandstone, sandstone of all shades and consistencies—white and yellow and gray and pink and red and maroon—some so friable that it could be crumbled into red dust, like that in the canyons of the Dirty Devil River, some so hard and durable that it gave the name to slickrock, like that which formed the towering maroon walls of the Escalante River canyons, sandstone found in what geologists call "formations"—the Kaiparowits Formation, the Dakota, the Entrada, the Wingate, the Carmel, the Navajo, the Kayenta, the Coconino, and half a dozen more placed in one of the arbitrary categories by which science has attempted to render comprehensible a couple of billion years of inhuman time.

It is not done, this work of shaping and carving and tearing down. The plateau still rises, the rivers still move through the land with their burden of time. They move that burden more slowly now, however, being encumbered by obstacles called dams, into whose reservoirs the rivers are forced to drop their multicolored loads of sands and silts, making new layers of sediment that someday will become stone. This is a temporary condition. It will not be long, as geology measures time, before the reservoirs are silted up to their brims and the rivers will begin to curl over the narrow concrete lips of the dams and continue their work. The plateau country, like the rest of our lovely, mutable planet, will always be caught in the act of becoming.

WHILE IT IS GENERALLY AGREED that the Colorado Plateau includes portions of Colorado, New Mexico, and Arizona, in no other part of any other state are its complexity and time-constructed beauty illuminated more brilliantly than in the wildlands of southern Utah. Colorado may have the Black Canyon of the Gunnison, New Mexico the spectacular magmatic upheaval called Shiprock, and Arizona the Grand Canyon and most of Monument Valley, but none of these shareholders in the plateau's wild landscapes enjoys southern Utah's abundance—for its portion of the plateau country is not marked by one or two or even three or four scenic marvels but by an enormous kaleidoscope of geological diversity whose impact on the senses can set the mind to reeling with every turn.

Do I overstate my case? Consider one unrecovering addict's brief tour of just a few of the highlights of this country. Because I am concentrating on the unprotected lands of the region, this exegesis cheekily ignores a few of the area's icons, like the redrock fins, spires, and arches in Arches National Park or the stone bridges in Natural Bridges National Monument; it also stubbornly refuses to discuss anything having to do with what you can see and do while putt-putting around Lake Powell in a houseboat or on one of those little abominations called jet-skis. Still, this outline should provide a fair grasp of the diversity of southern Utah's landforms and at least some sense of the life they hold.

First, take a look at some of what lies in the southwestern corner of the state. East of Interstate 15, above the Hurricane Cliffs and the Vermilion Cliffs, you can find the Virgin River, whose tributaries have carved through the red-soiled and juniper-topped tableland south of the Markagunt Plateau, grinding their way down through sandstone and limestone formations ranging in color from dark red to dirty white, leaving behind the great jumble of huge stone monoliths and narrow slickrock canyons embraced within Zion National Park. To get an even better idea of just how much sedimentary rock has been eviscerated from the land by the force of water, move north from Zion, up to the top of the nine-thousand-foot-high Markagunt Plateau, where the isolated spires and fractured rock walls of Cedar Breaks National Monument form a multicolored cascade of stone just below dark green forests of ponderosa pine—or over to the top of Paunsaugunt Plateau to the east, nearly as high, where you can find the even more intricate erosional formations of Bryce Canyon National Park. Nearly two miles in altitude, each of these eroded heights of land demonstrates just how much will have been accomplished when moving water has reduced the Colorado Plateau to a sea-level flatland.

The Markagunt and Paunsaugunt Plateaus are part of the "Grand Staircase" of plateaus and cliffs (or monoclines) that descend more or less southwesterly from the eleven-thousand-foot-high elevations of the Sevier and Aquarius Plateaus all the way down to the five-thousand-foot Kanab Plateau, at the North Rim of the Grand Canyon, the various "stairsteps" including the Pink Cliffs, the White Cliffs, and the Vermilion Cliffs just above the Utah-Arizona line. To the east of the Paunsaugunt Plateau and below the Escalante Mountains on the southernmost edge of the Aquarius Plateau is yet another "step" in the Grand Staircase—one that comprises one of the largest, most remote, and least-known geographic areas in the entire Southwest. This is the Kaiparowits Plateau, an utterly wild triangle of about a thousand square miles (the equivalent size of Rhode Island), bounded on its western side by a twenty-five-mile-long serrated ridge called the Cockscomb, on its southeastern side by the border with Glen Canyon National Recreation Area, and on its northeastern side by Fifty-Mile Mountain, which ends abruptly in the fifteen-hundred-foot drop of the Straight Cliffs.

The plateau is poorly watered (while the Paria River flows year-round, the rest of its streams are intermittent and seasonal), but, because its elevation drops so swiftly from seven thousand feet in the north to two thousand feet in the south, even its seasonal creeks have had enough speed and power to create perhaps the single most complex system of erosion-sculptured mesas, tablelands, benchlands, and canyons found anywhere north of the Grand Canyon. Only a little of it has been explored by anyone, and to drive or walk alone seventy miles across its profoundly exposed benches and mesas on the sublimely unimproved Smoky Mountain Road or to crawl through the great confusion of its dozens of intricate canyons is to be given an object lesson in just how stark the term "solitude" can be made to seem.

A few miles to the northeast, across the rolling desert scrubland of
Harris Wash, is a more welcoming kind of wilderness, the gentle, well-
watered, and truly enchanting canyon country of the Escalante River
as it flows from the Aquarius Plateau sixty miles southeast through
Glen Canyon National Recreation Area to Lake Powell. I confess to
some prejudice here. After my introduction to the wildlands of
southern Utah in Water Canyon in 1986, it was to the Escalante River
that I next traveled, and ever since that first visit I have spent more
time exploring the network of canyons and hollows created by the
Escalante and its tributaries than I have any other part of the region.
The river tumbles down from sources in the Escalante Mountains
and on the Aquarius Plateau—sometimes in flash floods, whose
power is suggested by the amount of debris you can find collared
around riverside willows and cottonwoods strong enough to hold
fast against the screaming rush of water—cutting its way through a
buff-colored mantle of Navajo and Dakota sandstone, then even
more deeply into the sleek red masses of Wingate and Entrada, their
exposed faces streaked with "desert varnish," a thin layer of clay
turned almost black by the oxygenization of iron and manganese.
When not running between sheer red walls, the river curls through
large parklike spaces called hollows.

From the top of its highest sunstruck talus slopes to its moist,
shadowy streambanks, the Escalante drainage supports a riot of vegetation that includes all the species of plants typical of canyon country—ground-hugging prickly pear and hedgehog cactus; a variety of
grasses interspersed with sego lilies, Indian paintbrush, milk vetch,
lupine, bee plant, buffalo berry, globe mallow, wild onion, penstemon,
wild rose, desert marigold, and other flowers; clumps of shadscale and
salt brush, Mormon tea and soaptree, chokecherry and box elder;
groves of Frémont cottonwoods and desert willows and impenetra-

ble thickets of tamarisk (salt cedar), an introduced species that, like many exotic migrants, tends to choke out endemic growth; scattered junipers and piñon and the occasional ponderosa pine that has sprouted from a cone washed down from the mountains; and, finally, hillside orchards of head-high big sage, whose aroma remains as vivid in the memory as the sound of the river's conversation with the rocks.

The Escalante empties into Lake Powell about ten miles above the point where the San Juan River arm of the lake joins that of the Colorado River. East along the course of the San Juan is country almost as dry and wild and canyon-cut as that of the Kaiparowits Plateau, high mesa country sliced by creeks feeding into the deep, high-walled meanders of the big river flowing all the way from the San Juan Mountains of southern Colorado and northern New Mexico. It is here, between U.S. 163 and Utah 95 (the "Bicentennial Highway"), that you can find one of the most impressive monoclines in the West— Comb Ridge, whose western face presents a ninety-mile wall of six-hundred-foot cliffs running almost precisely north to south from the high plateaus west of the Abajo Mountains until they peter out just above the San Juan River. And below the sheer sandstone wall is Comb Wash, a wide swale that nourishes a celebration of plant life nearly as rich and various as that in the Escalante canyons.

Remarkable as it may be as a geological formation, Comb Ridge has nothing on the Waterpocket Fold, an even more spectacular monocline to the northeast of the Escalante River, this one stretching a hundred miles from Thousand Lake Mountain to Lake Powell. Composed largely of Wingate and Navajo sandstone, though interspersed with variously colored layers of mudstone, siltstone, shale, and limestones, the rocks of this monocline were lifted up and folded down so abruptly that they form an almost vertical drop of about a thousand feet on its northeastern flank, while erosion has created a labyrinth of canyons throughout its narrow length—and, in some of the softer stone, has worn depressions, or "pockets," capable of holding rainwater.

Among the most striking features of the highest portion of the ridge are huge, rounded humps of cream-colored Navajo sandstone that rise up from layers of red Wingate and are said to resemble the domes of state and national capitol buildings—hence Capitol Reef National Park. Standing at one of the park's highest points—at the Strike Valley Overlook, for example—and looking northeast across the toothlike parade of rocks in Oyster Shell Reef just below, you get an incomparable view of one of the bigger surprises of canyon country: the wintry-looking (and often snow-capped) Henry Mountains, three peaks (Mount Ellen, Mount Pennel, and Mount Hillers) that rise several thousand feet above a series of mesas, as if portions of the Rocky Mountains had been picked up whole and moved down to the middle of a desert plain. Unlike the Rockies, however—which are the result of crustal faulting and wrinkling—the Henrys, like Navajo Mountain, the La Sals, and the Abajos, are laccoliths, mute reminders of the power of the magma beneath the earth's crust, ready to shrug such unsuccessful volcanoes into the waiting sky at any time.

On the other side of the Henrys—where the big Hump of Bull Mountain, a smaller laccolith, nestles against the northeastern flank of Mount Ellen—lie the canyons of the Dirty Devil River, etched into the top of the Burr Desert, a rolling red plain carpeted in dusty green sage and juniper. There are deeper canyon systems in southern Utah, with much more powerful rivers doing the work. Just a little over thirty tortuous miles to the east, in Canyonlands National Park, for instance, where the Green and Colorado Rivers join to become a single, rapidly moving torrent, the water has sliced nearly three thousand feet through some three hundred million years of mostly red sandstone geology to create the heartstopping declivity of Cataract Canyon, while just north of the park the Green River has engraved the signature of its narrow meanders into the entrenched convolutions of Labyrinth Canyon—and, even farther north, the same river has split the Tavaputs Plateau clean in two with Desolation Canyon.

The Dirty Devil River—barely a foot deep except during the flood season and in any season moving with a dowager's speed—seems a poor cousin when compared to the Green and the Colorado, and the depth of its cutting falls several hundred feet short of what they have done. Still, the canyon system that this river and its few tributaries have gouged two thousand feet into the landscape has an attraction that is as compelling as it is peculiarly its own. Essentially, that uniqueness is a matter of aesthetics; the canyons of the Green and the Colorado are definitively awesome, breathtaking, even a little frightening, but one would not ordinarily be moved to call them aesthetically pleasing. Encountering them for the first time can be nearly as unsettling an experience as that which unnerved Coronado's men when they became the first Europeans to stumble on the Grand Canyon four-and-a-half centuries ago.

But the canyons of the Dirty Devil *are* pleasing to the eye and heart, even when first met. From Burr Point, eleven miles west of Utah 95, you can stand at the edge of "forty miles of outdoors" (to borrow a phrase from Wallace Stegner) and look upon a wide chasm through the heart of which the café-au-lait river flows gently, curving past sandy banks green with riverine vegetation. Above the river rise chocolate-colored talus slopes of crumbled rock and sand that rain, wind, and gravity have dribbled off the rusty redrock of mesas and benchlands, each rising at its own altitude so that you are presented not with a single wide plain but with many individual plains spreading randomly to the horizon. Into these mesas and benchlands inter-mittent streams have carved a wonderland of narrow, meandering, high-walled canyons that feed into the chasm that holds the Dirty Devil.

If, when you stand above portions of the Colorado or Green Rivers, you are transfixed by the sight of the abyss that falls away from your feet, at Burr Point, looking on what the Dirty Devil has made, your eye moves comfortably from one point to another: from that gentle curve of river to that sheer redrock cliff; from that bench split like a failed layer cake by two or three side canyons to that butte thrusting up like a thumb from the flatland around it; from that line of ledges that climbs the side of a cliff like a staircase to that wide stretch of riverbank as white as a freshly laundered sheet—and, if you are lucky, it is all laid out before you under a wide blue sky through which fleets of pillowlike clouds drift toward the faint blue tips of the La Sal Mountains, which on a clear day poke up like a rumor seventy miles to the northeast.

Finally, consider the San Rafael Swell, which, though geologically different, larger, and more accessible than the Kaiparowits Plateau, shares much of its individuality. Like the Rockies and the Uintas, the San Rafael Swell is the child of orogeny, a chunk of the Colorado Plateau that mountain-building forces lifted some fifteen hundred feet above the surrounding country, giving it something of the char-acter of an island. An enormous ragged oval some twenty-two hun-dred square miles in area, it rises just north of Capitol Reef National Park, bounded on the west by piñon- and juniper-spotted hills that ultimately rise another forty-five hundred feet to the peaks of the Fishlake Mountains, and on the east by an anticline called the San Rafael Reef, a fifty-mile line of sandstone lumps the color of ancient ivory that juts abruptly from the floor of the San Rafael Desert as if it were a wall protecting the sanctity of some medieval kingdom. The illusion is given startling credence when, driving south along Utah 24 on the way to or from Hanksville, you see a crenelated massif rising more than two thousand feet above the surrounding landscape just behind the ominous-looking ramparts of the reef. This is Temple Mountain, so-called for its clear resemblance to the big Mormon Temple in Salt Lake City, but it takes only a little squint of the eye and not much stretch of imagination to see it as some enormous Germanic castle.

In or near the narrow confines of the reef itself can be found numerous hoodoos and other weirdly eroded rocks, some of the most startling of which are protected in Goblin Valley State Park. But it is in the deeper interior of the swell that you find a country only a little less fantastic than the architecture of fairyland tales (it is no accident, after all, that one of the swell's interior canyon systems is called Sinbad Country). Everywhere one finds isolated buttes and mesas big enough to be given the respect their names suggest—Sids Mountain, Mexican Mountain, Black Mountain, Cedar Mountain. At its northern end, the swell is drained by the San Rafael River and its tributaries flowing southeast down from the high country to the west and northwest, and while the depth and width of what they have accomplished falls short of that done by the Dirty Devil River to the south, the canyons they have made are impressive enough to have been called a Little Grand Canyon. Farther south, Muddy Creek has carved a deep, ten-mile-long meandering slice into the mesa top so constricted that it is called the Narrows and rarely sees the sun.

Like most of the Kaiparowits Plateau, however, the most memorable characteristic of the San Rafael Swell is its stunning aridity. Whether it is experienced in the nearly barren red desert stretches of Reds Canyon or the Mussentuchit Badlands, along the rolling gray hillocks of crusted cryptogamic soil that surround Factory Butte, or between the redrock walls of some waterless slot canyon, the overwhelming sense you get in the San Rafael Swell is one of stone and dust and desiccation, as if it is here that the forces of creation have decided to demonstrate with special precision just how alien and fragile a thing life can be.

THE ARID, BROKEN, FALLING-DOWN COUNTRY of the Colorado Plateau does not give a gentle welcome to life anywhere, but life is here nevertheless, in abundance and variety, from the microscopic organisms in fragile soils to the ghostly shapes of mule deer hidden among the willows. In its rivers and its more ambitious creeks swim several native species of fish, including Utah and roundtail chubs, the humpbacked chub (listed as endangered by the U.S. Fish and Wildlife Service), and several varieties of dace and shiners, as well as Colorado cutthroat trout and Lahontan and greenback cutthroat trout, both of the latter two listed as threatened species. There are a few tiger salamanders and a lot of western toads found in moist places, while beaver are everywhere in any canyon that boasts a respectable stream. Western rattlesnakes, king snakes, gopher snakes, and garter snakes slither through the grasses and the ground-hugging cacti, and ground squirrels and several species of collared, eared, and horned lizards skitter over and under the rocks.

In addition to mule deer, the larger mammals include mountain lions, coyotes (God's dog), and desert bighorn sheep—shy, elusive, and everywhere threatened. Scattered flocks of cliff swallows swoop up under the lip of sandstone cliffs, while tiny canyon wrens grace the air with the descending notes of their song; the ubiquitous magpies flap in black-and-white semaphores of agitation from tree to tree. Noisy crows and the occasional raven appear like smears of ink against the sky; pencil-legged great blue herons stalk the shallows with angular grace. Golden eagles and several species of hawks circle high above the canyons, and with the first shadow of night, hungry owls begin their silent flights in search of luckless rodents.

Adaptation and accommodation, the survival tools of evolution, have served the creatures of the canyon country well over the millions of years it has taken them to establish themselves here. Each species appears to have done so with a minimum of damage to habitat and little impact on the population of fellow species. While there is no real "balance" of nature in southern Utah or anywhere else (this little collection of ecosystems, like all ecosystems, is a dynamic entity that will see climates change, plant and animal populations shift, and species come and go over the eons), the relationships among all of the species have worked quite nicely for a long time now. They would likely continue to do so for another few millennia, were it not for the most recent addition to the mosaic of life here, one that threatens to destroy what time and evolution have contrived to make so splendid.

Looking toward Sams Mesa from Burr Point, in the proposed Dirty Devil
River Wilderness (1989)

Looking down on Smoky Mountain Road from the Kelly Grade,
Kaiparowits Plateau, in Grand Staircase–Escalante National Monument
(1998)

Looking up to the rim of Sams Mesa from the Dirty Devil River, in the
proposed Dirty Devil River Wilderness (1991)

Family Butte in winter, in the proposed San Rafael Swell Wilderness (1993)

Opposite Winter sky and mesa top in Sinbad Country, in the proposed San Rafael Swell Wilderness (1993)

Monolith, Arch Canyon, in the proposed San Juan–Anasazi Wilderness
(1992)

The moon setting over Factory Butte, in the proposed San Rafael Swell
Wilderness (1992)

A wall of goblins in Devil's Garden, off Hole-in-the-Rock Road, in Grand Staircase–Escalante National Monument (1998)

Opposite Looking to the rim of Smoky Mountain on the Kelly Grade, Kaiparowits Plateau, in Grand Staircase–Escalante National Monument (1998)

Stone goblins in Devil's Garden, in Grand Staircase–Escalante National
Monument (1998)

Escalante Arch in the proposed Escalante Canyons Wilderness, in
Grand Staircase–Escalante National Monument (1989)

Tomsich Butte, Reds Canyon, in the proposed San Rafael Swell
Wilderness (1992)

Sky over Harris Wash, off Hole-in-the-Rock Road, in Grand Staircase–
Escalante National Monument (1992)

PART TWO: THE PEOPLE

LIKE MANY MODERN PILGRIMS to the geological wreckage of southern Utah, I sometimes find myself giving way to the notion that my own feet are the first to have trod this or that piece of ground. It is hard not to fall victim to such prideful self-deceptions, particularly when you are on a solitary excursion. The land itself tends to collaborate in the delusion, as much of it appears to be devoid of human life and thus seems a great emptiness presented to you alone. And who wouldn't want to be the first human to stumble into the mouth of a slot canyon along, say, the Dirty Devil River, pushing past wispy desert willow branches and following a sandy track deeper and deeper into the secret dark place until you are squeezed between walls so narrow that you can only stand and stare up at a slender blue ribbon of sky winking at you from between stone walls three or four hundred feet high? Or to be the first to sit on a lip of rock, watching the San Rafael River curling its way through the layers of the San Rafael Swell while a hawk slowly circles up from the canyon bottom, higher and higher with every turn, until it is lost in the glare of the sun? There is a terrible need in such moments to emphasize your solitude by invoking the great I Am of discovery.

Some human was the first to be here or there in southern Utah, of course, but I have long since accepted that it was not me. The books tell me so, but there are other, more forceful ways of learning it, too. During my first solitary hike into the Escalante Canyons some years ago, I found myself wallowing in the notion of my uniqueness until I stopped by the side of a little creek to take a drink from my canteen (the canteen dates me, I know; I am a child of the war surplus years). My head tilted back to drink, my glance fell upon a huge, flat slab of stone sitting at the top of a talus pile across the river. The block appeared to have split off from the slickrock face of the cliff rising high above it. For reasons I still do not understand, I felt compelled to see what was behind the stone. I waded across the river and scrambled up the slope. And there, etched into and painted on the dark desert varnish of the cliff wall hidden by the great stone, I found a prehistoric gallery of petroglyphs and pictographs—stylized renderings of snakes and desert bighorn sheep, geometric designs whose cabalistic meanings were indecipherable, large-bodied figures with what appeared to be human heads. Whatever else these ancient scribblings might have been saying, their most compelling message was clear enough for even me to understand: *We were here first.*

These first arrivals were the Anasazi, which translates variously from the Navajo as "the ancient ones" or the "old enemies"—though the preferred academic term these days appears to be "pre-Puebloan people." Since I am an uncredentialed academic, I will continue to call them Anasazi. Under whatever name they traveled, their message is found everywhere in canyon country, from the infrequently explored Maze in Canyonlands National Park to the overvisited ruins of Grand Gulch Primitive Area south of the Hole-in-the-Rock Trail. For all its wildness and natural complexity, southern Utah is an enormous storehouse of human experience; square mile for square mile, it probably contains a greater abundance of archeological treasures than any other single part of any other single state in the West. Indeed, probably one of the reasons they fascinate us, these bits and pieces of a culture that began to flourish when Europeans were still worshipping entrails, is because they *are* everywhere. "In the last analysis," David Roberts writes in his wonderful book, *In Search of the Old Ones*, "the most impressive thing about the Anasazi is not their dazzling achievements at Cliff Palace, Pueblo Bonito, Hovenweep, and other storied cities of the dead. It is their thorough permeation of a country so difficult to travel in today that most of it remains uninhabited. Yet everywhere you go, in the most remote and unpromising corners of that country, you find a scattering of flint flakes here, a sherd or two of gray utilitarian cookware there, to testify to the passage of the ancients." How could a culture so widely scattered and so deeply embedded in the landscape, we wonder, be so completely gone? Where did it go? Where did it come from in the first place?

Archeologists have been trying to piece together this puzzle ever since the first Anasazi ruins began to fascinate Anglos in the last third of the nineteenth century, when clumsy and unenlightened ethnologists looted and desecrated hundreds of ancient sites in the name of science. Modern investigators are more sensitive about such things, but they are still diligently rooting around in the detritus of the past. Specialists calculate antiquity through advanced tree-ring and carbon 14 dating techniques, compare artistic patterns on surviving baskets and pottery, track hydrological cycles, and analyze the cabalistic meanings of petroglyphs and pictographs—all of this going on while modern looters, more interested in profit than in knowledge, still dig and vandalize, stealing pots and other artifacts, which can be sold to those dealers in southwestern art who do not question their suppliers too closely about the origins of the stuff, and blasting stones apart so that rock art can be shaped into coffee tables and mantelpieces.

While all the sophisticated rummaging has not yet given science a precise knowledge of how the Anasazi originated, where and how they lived, and when and why they left, the general outlines of the story are pretty well established by now and have been offered up in exquisite detail in mountains of monographs, conference papers, articles, and books. Me, I like the way the Hopi tell it. If their information is more metaphorical than anthropological, it still carries its own measure of truth—and makes for superior storytelling. In *Hotevilla: Hopi Shrine of the Covenant*, Thomas E. Mails and Dan Evehema offer the tale recounted by Hopi elder Dan Katchongva of the village of Hotevilla on the Third Mesa of the Hopi Reservation, pocketed in the heart of the Navajo Nation (a situation that pleases neither Hopi nor Navajo). For many Hopi, Hotevilla is an especially important holy spot, the dwelling place of those who have carried the traditions of their people longer and more faithfully than most. Until his death in 1972 (he was said to be at least 107 years old), Katchongva, a member of the Sun Clan, was one of the most revered of the elders, one of the few who knew firsthand some of the oldest mythic traditions of the Hopi.

For many generations, the first people had lived in peace and happiness beneath the surface of the earth, Katchongva said, a paradise given them by the Great Spirit, Maasaw. In exchange, the people had accepted a covenant with the supreme being, promising to obey his instructions. But Maasaw had created the people with divided spirits—the left side of each person, where the heart lay, was the good side; the right, away from the heart, was the bad side. The two sides warred against each other, and eventually the right side began to

45

dominate most of the people. They became materialistic, sexually promiscuous, and out of control.

The high priests gathered to seek a solution. Perhaps the best thing to do, they decided, was for the people to move to another world to start life all over again, this time holding to the old ways and honoring the holy traditions. For generations, they had heard sounds coming from above, up on the unseen surface of the earth. They decided to seek permission from that unknown being for the people to come to the surface for their regeneration. To investigate, they sent a swallow, a hawk, and a mockingbird. Only the mockingbird made it to the top, where he found Maasaw himself. "Why are you here?" the Great Spirit asked archly. "Could it be important?"

"Yes," the mockingbird replied. "I was sent here by the underworld people. They wish to come to your land and live with you, for their ways have become corrupted."

Maasaw gave his permission, but getting to the new world was not an easy thing to do. Somehow they had to get through the hard "sky" of their own world to get to the surface. They planted a spruce tree, hoping it would grow through the sky and provide a way, but its branches bent when the tree reached the top. A pine tree produced the same result. But then they planted a reed. Its sharp tip pierced the sky, and the people made their way to the surface by climbing up the inside of the reed itself.

On top, they found a beautiful, fertile land. But before they could be allowed to live with him, Maasaw said, they must first prove their faithfulness. He laid ears of corn before them. The ears were of various sizes. The people divided themselves into bands, and the leader of each band chose one of the ears of corn, most taking the longest ear they could get. But not one leader; he immediately chose the smallest ear. Maasaw then named each of the bands and gave them languages. The band whose leader, in his humility, had chosen the smallest ear of corn was called Hopi, a name that had special significance, Katchongva said, for it meant "not only to be peaceful, but to obey and have faith in the instructions of the Great Spirit, and not to distort any of his teachings for influence or power, or in any way to corrupt the Hopi way of life. Otherwise the name will be taken away."

After the gifts of corn, names, and languages were presented, Maasaw sent the people out to "the four corners of the new land," instructing them to put down cultural roots everywhere and to leave "many footprints, rock writings, and ruins, for in time many would forget that they were all one, united by a single purpose in coming up through the reed. Now that we were on top we were each to follow our own leaders, but so long as we did not forget the instructions of the Great Spirit we would be able to survive." Ultimately, Maasaw promised, the great migration would end and he and the people would meet again.

Many of the migrating people did forget the renewed covenant with Maasaw, but not the Hopi, who held true to the obligations that came with their name. And when the promised second meeting with Maasaw took place at Old Oraibi on Third Mesa, many thousands of years after the migration began, the faithful came to the spot from all over the land, abandoning their ancient settlements and beginning a new phase in the covenant with the Great Spirit. They could live with him, Maasaw said, but they must do so in the ways he gave them: "It is up to you," the Great Spirit said. "I have nothing here. My life is simple. All I have is my planting stick and my corn. If you are willing to live as I do, and follow my instructions, the life plan which I shall give you, you may live here with me and take care of the land. Then you shall have a long, happy, fruitful life." Those who accepted this new commitment to the covenant settled now in pueblos, not only on the mesas of what would become the Hopi Reservation, but also in river valleys and mesa tops throughout the Four Corners region, all the way to the valley of the Rio Grande. And in many of these same pueblos, traditional Hopi and Pueblo Indians still hold true to the meaning of the covenant with Maasaw, which began in the underworld millennia ago.

That, at least, is how Katchongva told it. Some archeologists question the reliability of the Hopi oral tradition, citing too many disruptive contacts and conflicts with other cultures, both Native American and European, for the stories to be acceptable even as metaphorical history. The similarities between much of Katchongva's recitation and biblical tales in Genesis and Exodus, for example, are striking. Even so, Katchongva's narrative, which presumably evolved before modern archeology began developing its own theories, still parallels with uncanny precision much of what modern science thinks it knows about the comings and goings of the Anasazi.

Anywhere from twenty thousand to ten thousand years ago, it is now believed, the Southwest began to be inhabited by bands of Paleo-Indian migrants who had drifted into the region from various points over several millennia, descendants of those original Americans who had crossed over to Alaska on the Bering "Land Bridge" from Siberia. They were hunters, these people, using atlatls to hurl spears tipped with quartzite or obsidian points at mammoths, camels, huge ancestral bison, and even an early species of horse. About six thousand years ago, when such large animals began to fade from the scene, either because of overhunting or climate change (or a combination of both), gathering began to be as important as hunting in the survival culture of these small bands of Archaic people. It was during this era that graffiti began to be pecked into the dark finish of desert varnish throughout the region, perhaps as a means of staking claim to hunting and gathering areas, warning other bands off, or propitiating whatever gods they may have worshiped—or just feared.

Some three thousand years ago the people began to cultivate corn, or maize, which apparently had found its way into the Southwest from South America, Central America, and Mexico through cultural interchange; corn was soon supplemented by beans and squash, which, with the occasional piece of meat from rabbits, squirrels, deer, and desert bighorn sheep, made for a rich and balanced diet. While still wandering considerable distances to forage and hunt, the people tended to settle now, working their fields, building the first small diversions to bring water to their crops, erecting granaries for storage on mesa tops or beneath the lips of cliffs. They dug pit houses in which to live and worship and began to make baskets, thereby earning their archeological designation as "Basketmakers" over succeeding periods of social evolution. With each period, the people became more sedentary, more complex in their social structure, and more sophisticated in their basketmaking efforts.

Then, beginning sometime in the eighth century, typical settlements gradually changed. Enclaves proliferated on or in nearly every available mesa top and canyon. Villages once characterized by disconnected structures became coherent earthen complexes, stone walls added to stone walls, houses connected to houses, often piled one upon the other like rooms in a prehistoric version of a condominium complex. Pit houses became bigger and deeper and more clearly revealed (if still poorly understood today) as places of communal worship, not unlike the kivas of the modern Hopi and other Pueblo people. Trails to and from fields and holy places became almost wide enough to be called roads; irrigation works grew larger and more complex; pottery began to supplement and then supplant basketmaking; rock art became more intricate and thoughtful. This was the Pueblo period, which truly began to flourish in the tenth century, when the climate improved and rainfall increased. Over the next three hundred years or thereabouts, the people thrived. Populations grew. Major settlements, satellite communities, and religious sites popped up everywhere in the Four Corners region—Grand Gulch, Mesa Verde, Butler Wash, Hovenweep, Betatakin, Canyon de Chelly, Chaco Canyon, and dozens more.

A true civilization had been implanted on the land, as surely as the Sumerians had conquered and overrun the Fertile Crescent, watered by the Tigris and the Euphrates Rivers four thousand years before Christ. But this civilization did not last even as long as that of the Sumerians. Beginning some time in the thirteenth century, the Anasazi began to leave their communities, many drifting east and commingling with other cultures, eventually becoming part of the modern Pueblo Indians of New Mexico. Others moved south, down to the mesas of the southern plateau, where they became identified as the Hopi. We still do not know precisely why they left. Climate change probably produced extended periods of drought, making it increasingly difficult to grow enough crops to sustain a burgeoning population. Even without water shortages, population growth may have become intolerable in many of the communities, leading to social conflicts, psychological pressures, and disease. Competition with belligerent, nomadic bands of Utes, it is fairly certain, made life more and more difficult and may explain why so many villages of the later Pueblo period were established high in the walls of cliffs, where they could more easily be defended; in time, these aggressive invaders might have been too much for the Anasazi to resist. For whatever reason or combination of reasons, the exodus took place so completely and over so wide a territory that we now call it the great abandonment, and by the middle of the fourteenth century it was complete.

Over the course of a few decades, then, the land of southern Utah was left to the wind and the silence, the people who once had called it home leaving behind only the disintegrating ruins of their mesa-top villages and sacred sites, their complicated irrigation systems, their granaries tucked into canyon walls, their cliff dwellings shadowed in the protective, overarching rock, their hundreds of thousands of incisions and paintings—a literature of stone no less eloquent for its still undecoded mystery. In the two or three centuries after the abandonment, Ute and Paiute Indians became the principal Native American inheritors of southern Utah. At no time were they so ubiquitous as the ancient ones, however, and being seminomadic peoples they left almost no marks of their presence on the land—save for the occasional addendum inscribed or painted on many of the petroglyph and pictograph galleries of the Anasazi, as if the Indians were bringing things up to date. Perhaps they were.

By then, representatives of another culture had come and gone in southern Utah, leaving even fewer marks of their passage than those of the Utes and Paiutes, though they had the furious energy of a great and glorious ambition behind them. While Arizona, New Mexico, and much of Colorado and Nevada have been pocked with hundreds of Spanish place names, all but a handful of sites and towns in southern Utah either are Indian or Anglo-Saxon in origin. Those few Spanish names that do exist can be attributed to the only serious expedition ever launched into the region by Spain's minions—and even then the expedition's members looked upon Utah as a place whose only virtue was that it might provide a convenient route to some-place else. Like much in the Spanish experience in the American Southwest, this hope became a great disappointment.

Back in the middle of the sixteenth century, after all, an expedition led by Francisco Vásquez de Coronado had spent nearly two years mucking about in Arizona, New Mexico, Texas, Oklahoma, and even Kansas in search of the treasure-rich Seven Cities of Cíbola and the great land of Quivira, where the streets were said to be paved with gold and the trees to be hung with golden bells whose rich tinkling lulled the happy residents to sleep in the afternoons. The expedition found no streets of gold, no tinkling bells in the scattered and some-times rebellious settlements of the Zuñi, Hopi, and other Pueblo In-dians, though Coronado's men killed and looted assiduously in their search for them. A subsidiary expedition sent west from the Zuñi set-tlements did discover the Colorado River and the Grand Canyon in 1540, but the space and depth of this great chasm merely befuddled and astonished the explorers, since there had been nothing in the Eu-ropean experience to prepare them for such a phenomenon. And they found no gold there, either.

While a few later expeditions tried to discover that which had evaded Coronado and his men, they were no more successful, and it was another fifty-five years before Don Juan de Oñate y Salazar led another major thrust into the land now called Nuevo México. He was not there in search of gold, though he would have been happy to find some, but to seize this land for King Philip, pinning down Spain's claim to most of the trans-Mississippi West and presumably blocking the rival continental hopes of England and France. And so it was that Oñate stood on the banks of the Rio Grande to proclaim—as quoted in Bernard L. Fontana's *Entrada: The Legacy of Spain and*

Mexico in the United States—with breathtaking bureaucratic arrogance that he was taking all

> tenancy and possession real and actual, civil and natural ... without excepting anything and without limitations, including the mountains, rivers, valleys, meadows, pastures, and waters. In [the king's] name I also take possession of all the other lands, pueblos, cities, towns, castles, fortified and unfortified houses which are now established in the kingdoms and provinces of Nuevo México, those neighboring and adjacent thereto, and those which may be established in the future, together with their mountains, rivers, fisheries, waters, pastures, valleys, meadows, springs, and ores of gold, silver, copper, mercury, tin, iron, precious stones, salt ... alum, and all the lodes of whatever sort, quality, or condition they may be, together with the native Indians in each and every one of the provinces, with civil and criminal jurisdiction, power of life and death, over high and low, from the leaves of the trees in the forest to the stones and sands of the river, and from the stones and sands of the river to the leaves in the forest.

Oñate and those who followed him succeeded in colonizing the valley of the Rio Grande—only to be thrown out during the great Pueblo uprising of 1680. A second effort, launched twelve years later, proved more durable, and over the next century and a half the Spanish built their own adobe civilization in the valley of the Rio Grande, then along the few rivercourses of southern Arizona, and finally in the rich coastal valleys of California. It was to establish a communications route between Santa Fe in New Mexico and Monterey in California, as it happened, that two priests, Francisco Silvestre Escalante and

Francisco Atanasio Domínguez were inspired to head out from Santa Fe in July of 1776 with eight soldiers and a full load of ignorance, bound for California but fated never to see it.

They traveled north first, up into western Colorado as far as the White River, then turned west along the southern flanks of the Uinta Mountains. Encountering the Green River, which they christened the Buenaventura with fine religious optimism, they crossed it and followed the course of the Duchesne and Strawberry Rivers, getting through the lower reaches of the Wasatch Range into the Utah Valley via Spanish Fork Canyon. They resisted the temptation to investigate the rumors of a huge salt lake to the north, seeking instead to find a viable route across the West Desert region. In October, while camped on the banks of Beaver Creek, they gave it up. Winter would soon be approaching, and God only knew what obstacles might await them.

They went south now, wandering all the way to the Virgin River, then crossing it and staggering east through the wilderness above the Arizona border, past Zion Canyon, the Vermilion Cliffs, the White Cliffs, the Escalante Mountains, and the splendid desolation of the Kaiparowits Plateau, before encountering the Colorado River at Padre Canyon. To get down to the river, they had to hack steps for themselves and their animals into the canyon walls, and once at the river it took some time before they found a fordable spot. Here, at the Crossing of the Fathers, they finally were able to slog through the river and begin the last leg of their return journey to Santa Fe, all the while "singing praises to God, our Lord," Escalante wrote in his report of the adventure, "and discharging some muskets in sign of the great joy that we all felt at having conquered so great a difficulty."

ESCALANTE AND DOMÍNGUEZ petitioned their superiors to establish a mission among the Indians they had encountered in the Utah Valley, but in vain. For the next seventy years, while the Spanish empire in the New World slowly disintegrated and finally collapsed in the Mexican Revolution of 1821, Utah remained the unsullied province of Indians. The region's only significant non-Indian presence in those years was that of the occasional mountain man, the West's first entrepreneur, wandering in and out of some of the river valleys of Utah in the 1830s in search of beaver pelts to be harvested and hauled back to the annual "rendezvous" on the Green River in Wyoming and from there to the trading centers of Taos and Bent's Fort in New Mexico or St. Louis in Missouri. The trade swiftly declined after hat fashions shifted from beaver fur to felt and silk. Even when Utah, with the rest of the Southwest, was taken from Mexico by the United States during the Mexican War of 1846–48, the region seemed fated to remain a blank in the settlement of the West.

But fate had to deal with the likes of Brigham Young and the unearthly perseverance of the members of the Church of Jesus Christ of Latter-day Saints—the Mormons. Their faith was founded in the upstate New York hamlet of Palmyra by Prophet Joseph Smith in 1830, but it did not prosper. The clannish, assertive, and frequently beleaguered Mormons had been driven out of Fayette, Ohio, in 1831 and then out of Kirtland, Ohio, in 1837, while their missionaries were attacked violently in Missouri. In 1837, they settled in Commerce, Illinois, on the site of which they built a new Zion called Nauvoo. Even here, however, violence between Mormons and "gentiles," as non-Mormons were described, continued. Finally, in a statement deemed so essential to the state's history that it was cited even in *Utah: A Guide to the State*, one of the guidebooks produced under the aegis of the WPA's Federal Writers' Project in the 1930s, Joseph Smith instructed the Quorum of the Twelve Apostles, the governing body of the church, to look to California and Oregon to "hunt out a good location, where we can remove to . . . and where we can build a city in a day, and have a government of our own, get up into the mountains where the Devil cannot dig us out, and live in a healthy climate, where we can live as old as we have mind to."

Before Brigham Young, president of the Quorum of Twelve, could get things under way, gentile officials arrested Smith in June of 1844, and when the Prophet was killed by a mob during an attack on the jail, leadership of the church fell to Young. In the fall of 1845, Young announced that he would bring his people out of the wilderness of Illinois and into yet another Zion somewhere in the West; true to his word, in January of 1847 he led an advance party across the Great Plains from their winter quarters on the banks of the Missouri River at Council Bluffs. In July, the party arrived in the valley of Great Salt Lake, where, so legend has it, a sick Young rose from his pallet in the bed of a wagon to proclaim, "This is the place." Members of the advance party began plowing the land along City Creek almost immediately. Over the next several years the new settlement blossomed into a major city, as thousands of Saints came streaming west, most from winter quarters and other points of the United States, but many from England, Wales, Denmark, and other European countries where the missionary zeal of the Mormons had fired religious imaginations.

The new Zion was called Deseret, and to provide for its rule the people made a new government, as the Prophet had ordered. Unfortunately, the state of Deseret had been carved out of federal land without regard for the niceties of federal law, which insisted that it actually was a territory of the United States and was to be called Utah. The government sent troops out to enforce federal sovereignty in 1857, but in the spring of 1858, before what was called the "Utah War" could become a war in fact as well as name, Young and federal authorities reached a compromise that kept Young in place as governor of the territory while the church conceded that the territory he governed was an entity of the United States.

Federal sovereignty or no federal sovereignty, Utah remained something of a theocracy, since the overwhelming predominance of Saints in the territory's population gave the church virtual rule over everything except U.S. military forces and federal district courts. Nor was its dominion felt only in Salt Lake City and its environs. The settlers of 1847 had hardly planted their first crop of potatoes before Young encouraged the formation of cooperative groups to spread the presence of the church into every available nook and cranny of Zion. By 1855, Wallace Stegner wrote in *Mormon Country*, Young

had virtually taken possession of a territory larger than Texas. He had spread the towns out from Salt Lake City through Salt Lake and Weber valleys, reached down into Utah Valley, jumped the Wasatch to colonize Sanpete Valley southeast of Salt Lake. He had planted a precarious outpost on the Colorado River at what is now Moab, had overleaped the Weber Valley settlements by two hundred and fifty miles to establish a mission colony at Fort Lemhi in the Salmon River Mountains of Idaho. . . . He had sprung clear across the Great Basin deserts to locate the Mormon Station, now Genoa, under the shadow of the Sierra on the emigrant road to California.

And, Stegner might have added, Young had also moved down the soil-rich valley of the Sevier River along what would become U.S. 89, where the hamlets of Fairview, Mt. Pleasant, Ephraim, and Manti sprouted, and then southwest down the Mormon Trail, which followed the line of what would become Interstate 15, where such unlikely settlements as Fillmore, Cedar City, Harmony, Santa Clara, and

Las Vegas challenged the desert landscape. In fact, Young tried to send his people all the way down the trail to the Pacific Ocean, where he aimed to establish a settlement. Los Angeles was in the way, so in 1851 he had to settle for San Bernardino, near the site of a sleepy old Spanish-Mexican pueblo seventy miles from the rolling white combers of the Pacific.

This energetic colonizing was challenged now and again by raiding parties of resident Ute Indians—particularly in Moab, where settlers were driven away entirely, not to return again until 1876—but resistance was effectively ended with the conclusion of the Black Hawk War of 1865–68. While the occasional "depredation" (as whites tended to view native resistance) still made life interesting in some areas for another ten years or so, by 1870 most of the Utes were settled on what would become the Uintah and Ouray Indian Reservation in the north central portion of the state, left to the tender mercies of the Bureau of Indian Affairs. Even before the uneasy peace with the Utes had been established, colonizers had drifted into the southernmost valleys of the state, and now the pattern continued, a scattering of little farming and ranching communities springing up just about anywhere that land and water combined to make settlement feasible.

Holding down the northwestern corner of the ragged topographic square of southern Utah was Castle Dale, founded in 1875 on the northern edge of the San Rafael Swell, where in the 1880s and 1890s the complex landscape provided such superior hiding places for outlaws, including Butch Cassidy and the Sundance Kid, that it became known as Robbers Roost. Two hundred miles to the southeast, Bluff, on the San Juan River, pinned down the southeastern corner in 1880—though not before intrepid Saints were forced to construct a road through the wilderness from Escalante to the redrock bluffs above the Colorado River, and, once there, to carve a primitive trail for their wagons down a canyon so precipitous and narrow as to be little more than a hole in the rock (remnants of both Hole-in-the-Rock Road and the canyon descent remain and have become minor tourist attractions). In the northeast corner sat Moab, on the Colorado River, just a few dozen miles from the Colorado border. After its resettlement in 1876, the little town in the Spanish Valley soon became the largest community south of the Tavaputs Plateau. And in the southwest corner, where the plateau country mingled with the Great Basin and Mojave Deserts, there was St. George, founded in 1861 and named after one of Brigham Young's principal advisers, George Albert Smith. (Catholics had official saints, the town's slightly irreverent founders reasoned, so why not Mormons?)

By the turn of the twentieth century, the thousands of square miles of canyon country between these points were pockmarked by towns with names like Green River, Emery, Koosharem, Loa, Torrey, Bicknell, Caineville, Hanksville, Notom, Fruita, Boulder, Escalante, Monticello, Blanding, and Kanab. They were quiet villages whose graceful presence on the land seemed to embody everything noble that human beings hoped to find in the communal dream of Arcadia. Most were surrounded by irrigated fields that seemed even more astonishingly verdant when viewed against the starkly beautiful redrock of the landscape. Each was blessed by the wide streets proclaimed by Mormon tradition. Most featured Mormon ward houses for public meetings and community entertainment (dancing and singing were always big among the Mormons), and while some eventually contained enough gentiles to warrant a standard Protestant or Catholic church here and there, these structures were put in the shade by what was always the most imposing building in town—the local Mormon chapel (though Manti and St. George were prosperous enough to have erected ambitious temples after the fashion of the great temple in Salt Lake City, their ethereal white spires still visible for miles as they rise majestically above the modest houses and wide streets of their towns). While the headquarters church in Salt Lake City, hungry for respectability and acceptance, would ban the practice of polygamy in 1896 in exchange for statehood, in many of the tidy, hermetic villages of southern Utah there still would be more wives than husbands for many years.

Pious, sturdy, hardworking, isolated, and comfortable in the assurance of heaven, the Mormon settlers of southern Utah were given the benediction of seven decades or so before the pressures of an increasingly complex world rudely assaulted the assumptions and traditions of their peaceable kingdom.

For the most part, southern Utah escaped the disruptive excitements brought by the nineteenth-century mining industry, which had exploded throughout the Rocky Mountain region in the 1860s and 1870s. Once the amount of gold in California had been exceeded by the number of those looking for it after the great rush of 1849–52, "Old Californians" had overrun the intermontane West like vagrant conquistadors in search of treasures of gold and silver. They had found it, too, though some of the treasure was copper and almost all of it was in lode form that required labor, capital, and technology to dig it out and refine it. By the 1870s, scores of the high mountain valleys and canyons of the Rockies reverberated to the ugly clatter of industrial mining, including those in the Wasatch Range and the Uintas of Utah, while in a place called Bingham Canyon, a few miles southwest of Salt Lake City, early deposits of lead and silver gave way to huge quantities of copper, the extraction of which produced one of the largest open-pit mines in the world.

While the relatively genteel arts of agriculture and free-range husbandry continued to provide most of southern Utah's economic base into the 1940s, it, too, had experienced a little of the raw energy of extraction. Deposits of what local Indians called "the rocks that burn" were discovered in the San Rafael Swell, and the town of Emery continued to produce respectable amounts of coal from small mines well into the twentieth century. The coal that underlay the plateau country to the north, however, was of generous quantity and even better quality than that of the Emery district, and by World War II the mines of Carbon County were producing more than five million tons of the stuff every year. While many of the Carbon County mines have long since gone bust, coal production is still a significant employer in the region.

More in line with traditional mining excitements was the experience in Silver Reef over on the Kolob Plateau northeast of St. George. Here, sandstone deposits of silver had been found in 1866, swiftly bringing in a small army of prospectors and speculators from Pioche and other mining districts in nearby Nevada. Within a few years, a smoking industrial mining camp had been established in the sandstone wilderness of the plateau, complete with all the transient clutter and bustle typical of such enterprises throughout the West. At its peak in the late 1870s, Silver Reef's biggest mines were producing anywhere from $300,000 to $500,000 worth of refined silver ingots every year. After 1893, when the U.S. government suspended silver purchases begun in 1873, the price of silver plummeted, production costs rose, and while the district enjoyed a couple of brief recoveries, by 1903 it was all but dead.

If mining was a minor part of the region's economy, timber extraction from Dixie, Fishlake, and Manti–La Sal National Forests remained an almost invisible factor until after World War II, when the postwar boom in population and housing forged a nationwide symbiosis between the U.S. Forest Service and the timber industry, which systematically began stripping billions of board feet off the forests of the West every year—including millions of board feet of spruce, fir, aspen, and ponderosa pine taken from Boulder Mountain, Thousand-Lake Mountain, Blue Mountain, the La Sal Mountains, and other available peaks and slopes of southern Utah.

At the same time, the livestock industry began running more and more summer cattle on the government-permit grazing lands of the same mountains while spreading them through the fragile riparian areas of the lower river valleys during the rest of the year. Both practices added their own impact to the mix of pressures on the land (some environmentalist critics have been known to describe grazing as being as extractive as logging and at the extreme just as damaging). Tourism, meanwhile, which had been a minor consideration before the war, slowly began to take on some of the dimensions of the monster it would become, as a growing population of vacationers with postwar money to spend began bouncing over the region's still primitive highways and byways in increasing numbers.

Generally, however, southern Utah probably would have remained relatively unmarked by most of the careless enthusiasms that were transforming so much of the United States in the immediate postwar years had it not been for the dangerous protocols of the cold war. (It is perhaps ironic that a region so peculiarly isolated from much of the life of its own state, much less that of the whole country, should have been so vulnerable to events of truly international significance.)

In 1941, the authors of *Utah: A Guide to the State* casually mentioned that in some portions of the plateau country a few mines were producing "radioactive minerals containing uranium and vanadium" but gave the matter little attention. By the end of the war, few people—and certainly not the government of the United States—were so quick to dismiss the importance of those "radioactive minerals." America's nuclear arsenal needed them for the production of Uranium 235 and Uranium 238, the first for the making of simple atomic bombs, the second for the production of plutonium, the essential ingredient in the hydrogen bomb.

As early as 1948, the Atomic Energy Commission (AEC) offered to buy uranium ore over the next fourteen years for a minimum of $3 a ton, with a sliding scale of higher prices for higher-quality ore. What was more, it would prime the production pump by paying a bonus of no less than $15,000 and as much as $35,000—again, depending upon the quality—for the first five tons of uranium oxide produced from any mill until 1957. These were prices that challenged the best that gold and silver had returned in the glory years of nineteenth-century mining, but the common perception was that the United States had few significant deposits of uranium, and, even with the government's price incentives, exploration and production in the Colorado Plateau moved slowly for several years.

Then came Charles Augustus Steen, a poor geologist from Texas, who had started digging around in Big Indian Wash in the Lisbon Valley forty miles southeast of Moab in 1950. Steen staked out a claim and called it the Mi Vida, and on December 1, 1952, his drills bit into rock that assayed out with such a high percentage of uranium that he knew immediately that he was a rich man. "I can remember that night," he recalled, as reported in *Uranium Frenzy: Boom and Bust on the Colorado Plateau*, by Raye C. Ringholz. "My mother and I went down to Moab. It was about 10 o'clock and I had a quart of whiskey. We went to a hot dog stand where the bus station used to be. We were the only ones there. The whole town was locked up. That was the night of the discovery . . . and that was the last time that Moab went to sleep at 10 o'clock for a long time."

Meanwhile, a prospector named Vernon Pick announced that he had made a major strike at about the same time near Muddy Creek in the San Rafael Swell. He called his mine the Delta, and it was as rich a find as the Mi Vida. After hauling out a million dollars in ore in a matter of months, he sold the Delta to the Atlas Corporation for nine million dollars; Atlas promptly named it the Hidden Splendor.

This was the stuff of dreams, a phenomenon not unlike that of the original Gold Rush of 1849. Newspapers from San Francisco to New York City, as well as such national magazines as *Life*, *Look*, *Colliers*, the *Saturday Evening Post*, *Reader's Digest*, *McCall's*, and even that urbane sophisticate, the *New Yorker*, gave this curious new Golconda pages and pages of nearly hysterical coverage. While AEC geologists cruised over the plateau in airplanes equipped with scintillators for the detection of "hot spots," ten thousand former shoe clerks, dude ranch operators, cowboys, stockbrokers, garage mechanics, and other frenzied amateurs spilled throughout the Four Corners region, stumbling around in the wilderness equipped with little more than blind optimism and sundry electronic gadgets that whirred, clicked, buzzed, and beeped when in the presence of uranium—or so their manufacturers promised. "I started out from here with 400 pounds of equipment," New Jerseyite Joe Morris reported to the *New Yorker* from Moab, "a Geiger counter, an enormous pickaxe, two hammers, field glasses, a portable fluorescent lamp for testing samples, a mortar and pestle for pulverizing them, two big cameras, a sleeping bag, some canned goods, and half a dozen prospecting manuals. I had so many straps dangling around my neck that one false move and I'd have hanged myself."

Morris did not hang himself, but neither did he strike it rich. Few did, as was usually the case, but it did not matter much. With the government guaranteeing purchase and paying such good money, the dream was a long time dying. As Steen had suggested, Moab was transformed. The town already had achieved a minor level of fame as a service center for film companies shooting westerns in the surrounding landscape (*Rio Grande*, with John Wayne and Maureen O'Hara, was perhaps the best known), and the Moab Film Commission, formed in 1949 to promote the town and the region for such purposes, was the first such commission in the world.

Still, when Charlie Steen settled here and formed the UTEX Corporation as the corporate entity for the Mi Vida mine and other operations (today, his house, perched on a hill high above the town, has been converted into a locally renowned restaurant), Moab was transmogrified from a mildly active little country town into the "Uranium Capital of the World." Between March of 1952 and April of 1953, its population doubled; in a few months more, it had tripled, and by 1956 had nearly quadrupled. Sewage treatment facilities, housing, schools, hospitals, gas and electricity, telephones, water supplies— everything that went to make a functioning city—were inadequate. At one point, Richard A. Firmage reports in *A History of Grand County*, "school shifts had to have triple sessions, three students at times shared one desk, and twelve grades were housed in one building. To add to the already overloaded resources, the district also began to supply free lunches to school children, since so many were dependents of destitute prospectors scouring the countryside for that elusive bonanza strike." People lived in tent villages, chicken coops, abandoned sheds, or the backs of automobiles. More than half the families in town, the *Moab Times-Independent* reported on January 27, 1955, were inadequately housed. "Moab's backyard," one observer said, "strikes you as one vast trailer camp."

Meanwhile, the boom continued, the government purchasing nearly $150 million worth of uranium ore every year. "No Talk Under $1,000,000" read a sign at Moab's Uranium Club, where a fee of a hundred dollars got you in to have a drink. (There were no legitimate saloons in Utah in those days—only "clubs," in which "members" could be served liquor after the payment of dues; in Moab, as elsewhere, the device did not seem to slow consumption appreciably.) But you did not have to live in Moab to talk like a millionaire. In Salt Lake City, historian Larry Meyer wrote in the June/July 1981 issue of *American. Heritage*, there blossomed "a mad circus of speculation in penny stocks. . . . Twenty-four hours a day you could trade in such companies as El Dorado, Shamrock, or King Midas. No matter that the company was without claims, or that it had no intention of ever mining ore, lacking even a pick to dig it up or a wheelbarrow to put it in. On May 24, 1954, more shares were bought or sold over the counter in Salt Lake City than changed hands on the Big Board in New York." Hundreds of millions of dollars in uranium stocks crossed the counters of brokerage houses and the bars of "clubs." Claim disputes and outright swindles proliferated, and at least one murder was perpetrated in the name of greed. As described by Edward Abbey in *Desert Solitaire*, these were "years of feverish struggle, buying and selling, cheating and swindling, isolation, loneliness, hardship, danger, sudden fortune and sudden disaster."

And then it was done. After starting the whole thing with its open-handed generosity, the AEC proclaimed in 1957 that the government had almost all the uranium it needed, thank you very much, and that no ore would be purchased from any mines discovered after that year. No more bonuses, and, with a few exceptions—like that for Charlie Steen's URECO mill in Moab (later purchased by the Atlas Corporation)—no more guaranteed purchases of processed ore.

Prospecting died; Geiger counters were placed on closet shelves; deeds to undeveloped claims were tucked away in bureau drawers; a hundred paper millionaires were left with a wealth of, well, paper. The population of Moab began to decline, property values fell, and when Steen's Mi Vida mine shut down in 1964, it seemed to close the door to an era.

IN THE MID-1960S, after the first nuclear-powered generating plant at Shippingport, Pennsylvania, had proved out, a new use for uranium developed: while it might not be needed any longer for the destruction of cities in the Soviet Union, it would now light the cities of America. A much reduced version of the uranium rush of the 1950s developed, but this time it was dominated by big business, as Homestake, Union Carbide, Anaconda, Newmont, Phelps-Dodge, and other national corporations shouldered aside the small prospector and the smalltime operator in a pattern common to western mining for more than a century. And as the boom in nuclear power generation rose through the 1970s, then began to taper off and finally enter a period of decline when its dangers and its economic drawbacks became increasingly apparent, uranium mining and processing rose and fell with it. By the 1990s, uranium would provide only a tiny share of the region's economic pie.

The populations and property values of Moab and other towns that had been infected by both booms steadily fell. Even Charlie Steen ultimately went broke. Those who remained were left with colorful memories of exciting times. And, for too many, with something else. Back in 1952, the reader of an article on Vernon Pick in *Life* magazine wondered what the government might do for him: "My mother-in-law recently was subjected to intense radiation treatments," he said. "She's cured now—but—she gets a definite 'ping' from my counter. Now here is what I would like to know—how much will you offer per pound for her?"

Fifteen years later, the man's joke would have rung hollow. "More than a thousand uranium miners in this country can be expected to develop lung cancer by the end of 1985, according to a study now receiving highly restricted circulation in the Executive Branch of government," wrote reporter J. V. Reistrup in the *Washington Post* on April 4, 1967. "Another secret document charges that the radiation standards now under study for the mines are 'significantly inadequate' to keep the number from rising." Reistrup's story helped spur a twenty-five-year controversy, during which uranium-mining companies, uranium-mining states, and the U.S. government fought to escape being held responsible for such deaths and to avoid being forced to pay compensation to still-living victims or the families of those who died. This dark, stupid malevolence ended only when Congress passed the Radiation Exposure Compensation Act of 1990 and the truest victims of the great uranium rush finally got payment, as inadequate as it was late, for what they had lost in the dream that failed.

By then something else was at stake in southern Utah, something which, if lost, would have its own measure of sorrow. It was an idea, and it was called wilderness.

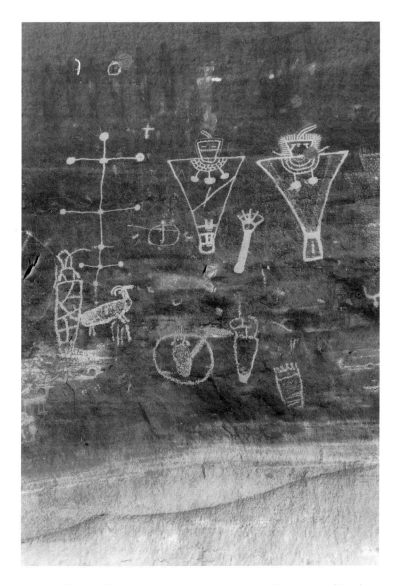

Petroglyphs and pictographs, Thompson Canyon, in the proposed Book
Cliffs–Desolation Canyon Wilderness (1990)

Anasazi ruins, Arch Canyon, in the proposed San Juan–Anasazi
Wilderness (1992)

Indian corn and metates, Sand Creek Canyon, in the proposed Escalante
Canyons Wilderness, in Grand Staircase–Escalante National Monument
(1990). The site has since been vandalized.

Mount Holmes in the Little Rockies, on Bureau of Land Management lands
in southern Utah (1990)

Opposite Dance Hall Rock, where Mormon pioneers capered and danced
during their trek in 1879 along Hole-in-the-Rock Road, in Grand Staircase–
Escalante National Monument (1998)

Burr Trail through Long Canyon, in Grand Staircase–Escalante National Monument (1989). Proposed wilderness lies on either side of the road.

Abandoned truck, Reds Canyon area, in the proposed San Rafael Swell
Wilderness (1992)

Abandoned stone structure outside Hanksville, Utah (1991)

Abandoned "Old West" movie town outside Old Paria, in Grand
Staircase–Escalante National Monument (1998)

Downtown Moab on Memorial Day (1998)

Opposite Solitary cottonwood, Paria River, in the proposed Kaiparowits Plateau Wilderness, in Grand Staircase–Escalante National Monument (1998)

Mormon Temple in Manti, Utah (1991)

Glen Canyon Dam, Page, Arizona (1998)

Shadow of the Bicentennial Highway Bridge over the Dirty Devil River
Canyon, submerged now under the waters of Lake Powell (1998)

PART THREE: THE PROBLEM

84   In 1931, an eighteen-year-old refugee from the depression-ridden
urban swarms of Los Angeles and San Francisco wandered into the
falling-down country of San Juan County, Utah. His name was Everett
Ruess, and he was but one among tens of thousands of young men
and women who hitchhiked, hopped the freights, or simply walked
from one place to another during these hard times, moving back and
forth across the continent like particles in liquid suspension, fleeing
the despair and desperate violence of the big cities or the parched
and withered land of farms and ranches gone broke, their families
wracked by sudden, inexplicable poverty. Most of these refugees were
looking for work, any kind of work, something that would validate
hope in a country gone tight with hopelessness.

   But not Everett Ruess. He was seeking something else, something
that lay close to the marrow of his being. Like many young people of
any era, he dreamed of translating beauty into art and literature that
would outlast him, and when he saw the redrock wilderness of southern Utah for the first time, he was beatified. Here, he believed, he had
found a home for dreams. For the next three years, he investigated

this new country on long solitary excursions, leaving little unseen and unexperienced. These were, he wrote, as reported in W. L. Rusho's biography, *Everett Ruess: A Vagabond for Beauty*, "the happiest days of my life," and his explorations "a beautiful dream, sometimes tranquil, sometimes fantastic, and with enough pain and tragedy to make the delights possible by contrast. . . . Beauty has always been my god; it has meant more than people to me. And how my god, or goddess, is flouted [*sic*] in this country which to me is the most beautiful I've known in all my wanderings!"

Everett Ruess was a pretty fair artist, and diligent practice might have made him a much better one, just as time and experience might have honed his endearing but callow effusions into literary respectability. Instead, like Judge Joseph Crater in 1930, he achieved immortality mainly by vanishing. On November 11, 1934, with two burros and a good stock of artist's supplies and food, Ruess left the town of Escalante for the last leg of an expedition that already had taken him from Kayenta and Gallup in New Mexico to Grand Canyon National Park in Arizona, then through Zion and Bryce Canyon National Parks in southwestern Utah before he ended up in the little cowtown under the Straight Cliffs. He might be heading down toward Monument Valley, he told friends in Escalante, or over to Marble Canyon, or perhaps he would end up in Boulder on the other side of Hells Backbone. "As to when I shall return to civilization," he wrote in a final letter to his brother, "it will not be soon, I think. I have not tired of the wilderness; rather, I enjoy its beauty and the vagrant life I lead, more keenly all the time. I prefer the saddle to the streetcar and star-sprinkled sky to a roof, the obscure and difficult trail, leading into the unknown, to any paved highway, and the deep peace of the wild to the discontent bred by cities. Do you blame me then for staying here, where I feel that I belong and am one with the world around me?" Except for a brief appearance at the confluence of the Escalante and Colorado Rivers eight days later, Ruess was never seen again.

And so he became legend, a name to be reckoned with, about which whole architectures of speculation were built as the decades passed. Perhaps he was murdered by Utes, the local folk would tell one another in the ward houses of the little Mormon settlements. Perhaps he was killed by prospectors on whose secret claims he had stumbled. Maybe it was suicide; artists were famous for that sort of thing, weren't they? More likely, some said, it was just a lonely death by accident, disease, thirst, or heatstroke. Others insisted that, like Joe Hill, Ruess had never died at all but was still wandering somewhere in the secret recesses of the Kaiparowits Plateau or the side canyons of the Escalante, stubbornly following the dream of beauty. "It is a nice thing to think about," Wallace Stegner wrote in *Mormon Country* in 1942, "that maybe tonight he is sitting under the shadow of some cliff watching the light race upward on the mountain slope facing him, trying to get it into water colors before the light leaves him entirely."

People continue to wonder about what happened to Everett Ruess, but few who know the story have any trouble understanding what it was that drove him into the wild country again and again, until it probably killed him He was plainly seduced by beauty so elemental, by space so profound, and by solitude so complete that it simply could not be resisted. While few people then or later were ever tempted to test fate quite so completely as Everett Ruess, there were many who found in the beauty, space, and solitude of this land something so precious that it must at all costs be saved from the worst that we and our society could do to it.

It was that passion that had already fired the efforts of a few enthusiasts to get some of the area's most important scenic areas protected. In 1909, California borax king Stephen Tyne Mather, who would become the first director of the National Park Service in 1916, joined his own influential voice to a small chorus that persuaded President Taft to establish Mukuntuweap National Monument in the southwestern part of the state; the name was changed to Zion in 1918, and in 1929 it was redesignated Zion National Park. Alexander Ringerhoffer, a Hungarian immigrant who prospected for a while in the magnificently sculptured redrock country near Moab, became so entranced with the region's exquisitely complex landforms that he managed to enlist the support of the Denver & Rio Grande Railway and L. L. ("Bish") Taylor, editor of the *Moab Times-Independent*, in a campaign to protect it; and in 1928, President Herbert Hoover established Arches National Monument (it became a national park in 1972).

Then there was Ruben C. Syrett, first postmaster of Bryce Canyon, who joined with the Utah Parks Company to get Bryce Canyon National Park designated in 1928, and Bishop Ephraim P. Pectol of Torrey in Wayne County, who, upon being elected to the state legislature in 1933, immediately petitioned Congress to establish what local folks called the "Wayne Wonderland" as Capitol Reef National Monument, the government finally complying with his wish in 1937 (the monument became a national park in 1971). None of these designations, however, came anywhere near the scope and audacity of an idea that started brewing in Washington, D.C., not long after the disappearance of Everett Ruess—and even if the proposal ultimately failed, it served nicely as the opening shot in what would become one of the most important environmental crusades in modern American history.

It began in 1936, when Interior Secretary Harold L. Ickes ordered the National Park Service to study the possibility of having President Franklin Roosevelt invoke the Antiquities Act of 1906 to establish a 4.4 million-acre Escalante National Monument that would include federal land on both sides of the Colorado River from the Vermilion Cliffs on the Arizona-Utah border to Labyrinth Canyon on the lower stem of the Green River. Ickes may well have been influenced in his thinking by Robert Marshall, a forester with a Ph.D. from Johns Hopkins who had been loaned to the Interior Department by the Forest Service in 1933 to supervise recreation and forest lands on sixteen Indian reservations and had become one of the interior secretary's closest government friends, as well as a useful ally. Marshall was a man with strong leanings toward the preservation of wild country in all its forms—in 1935 he cofounded the Wilderness Society—and one of his first acts in his new job at Interior was to promote the designation of more than four million acres of wilderness preserves on the reservations. In 1937, just after Marshall had returned to the Forest Service as head of recreation lands, Bureau of Indian Affairs head John Collier authorized the preserves (unfortunately, they were rescinded during the wilderness-unfriendly Eisenhower administration sixteen years later).

Even while he was staking out Indian wilderness, the irrepressible Marshall had launched a personal survey to discover the largest unroaded and undeveloped chunks of land in the rest of the forty-eight states, areas that he hoped would be the foundation for a national system of preserved wilderness. "The battle to protect the wilderness is a critical one," he wrote in the November 1936 issue of the *Living Wilderness*, publishing the preliminary results of the survey. "Definitely there have not been enough large roadless tracts safely reserved from invasions. There is important need to make a study . . . concerning which officially designated roadless areas should be enlarged, and which areas on which official action has not been taken should be established." Most of the potential enclaves Marshall had discovered were on national forest land, but among them were more than twelve million acres of unroaded wilderness areas in southern Utah, including those being studied by the National Park Service. It is difficult to believe that it was not Marshall himself who first brought this area to the attention of his friend and former boss, Ickes.

Marshall, sad to say, died in 1939, not long after the Escalante study was finished and the national monument proposal put into written form. Roosevelt, whose ideas of natural beauty were largely defined by the forest lands in which he had grown up in and around Hyde Park on the Hudson River in New York (and which he continued to nurture as a gifted, if amateur silviculturalist), had little affection for desert country. "It looks dead to me," he once said of the Grand Canyon. Nevertheless, had there been no significant opposition to the Escalante proposal in Congress or in Utah, FDR probably would have designated the monument without a second thought, just as he had the 330,689-acre Organ Pipe Cactus National Monument in Arizona in 1937. But there was considerable opposition, both in the state and in Congress, particularly among western congressmen and senators who controlled all committees devoted to western land matters and were unanimous in the conviction that a benevolent Providence had created these lands and given them to the nation mainly to promote the greater good and glory of the mining and livestock industries. The 241,904 acres set aside in Capitol Reef National Monument, together with those in the other park units of the region, they insisted, were quite enough southern Utah scenery removed from the free enterprise system. Secretary Ickes' proposal was whittled down to a compromise of 1.5 million acres, but even that proved to be more than the opposition was willing to swallow. With FDR's support, Ickes then had his department draft an amendment to the Antiquities Act that would allow the president to establish "national recreation areas" that would serve many of the same recreation purposes as national monuments but would specifically allow mining, water projects, grazing, and hunting. The anti-Escalante folk wanted nothing to do with this either, and shortly after its introduction, the amendment died in committee.

The Escalante National Monument was an idea whose time had not yet come. So was another Ickes proposal of 1939. He outlined the idea in a speech before California's Commonwealth Club in February of 1939, offering up the vision of a law that would empower the president to set aside portions of national parks and monuments as wilderness areas to be kept forever free of automobiles, roads, and any kind of commercial use. "In asking Congress for the passage of this bill to set aside wilderness areas," he said, "I am requesting that the discretionary power of my own Department be cut down. I suppose that is something new in the annals of government. . . . But that is what I desire. I want those wilderness areas so protected that neither I, nor any future Secretary of the Interior, can lower their guard merely by signing an administrative order."

If most western congressmen and senators had not liked the Escalante notion or the proposed amendment to the Antiquities Act, they cordially despised the wilderness idea. This bill, too, died in committee not long after its introduction in the Senate by Alva Adams of Colorado. But if the Ickes bill was moribund, the idea was not, and it was not long after the end of World War II that it rose up again, driven to the surface by the first major conservation skirmish to achieve national prominence since John Muir and the Sierra Club had lost their fight to keep a dam out of Yosemite National Park in 1913.

THIS BATTLE, TOO, was over dams. In 1950, Interior Secretary Oscar Chapman announced that the Bureau of Reclamation was ready to add a couple of other elements to the Colorado River Basin Project, an enterprise that had already plugged the Colorado with Boulder (later renamed Hoover), Parker, and Imperial Dams—in spite of the warnings given nearly seventy-five years before that the watershed of the Colorado could not be expected to fulfill the irrigation dreams of humankind indefinitely. The prophet of common sense had been Major John Wesley Powell, a largely self-taught government scientist who had been the first to lead a river expedition through the Grand Canyon, in 1869, then had launched a major survey of the Colorado Plateau. His conclusions as to the viability of the human settlement of a nearly rainless land were first presented in his *Report on the Lands of the Arid Region of the United States* in 1878, and as late as the 1890s he was still sounding the cry. When a meeting of irrigation enthusiasts met in 1893 to promote the "development" of the Colorado and its tributaries to transform "the desert into a garden of beauty," Powell stood up to warn them that "[you] are piling up a heritage of conflict . . . for there is not sufficient water to supply these lands. There is no water to put on half the lands now owned by the Government. There is not water enough in all the arid region to irrigate the lands which the Government has already disposed of." The irrigation boomers had ignored Powell's stark little jeremiad, going on to persuade Congress to create the Bureau of Reclamation in 1902, and it was the bureau that had gone on to launch the Colorado River Project.

Now, in 1950, the agency wanted to erect two more dams, at Echo Park and Split Mountain Canyon, on two of the Colorado's major tributaries, the Green and Yampa Rivers. Both dams would flood much of Dinosaur National Monument on the Utah-Colorado border. It would take a special act of Congress to approve such a desecration, and opposition to the idea was immediate and remarkably effective. "If Dinosaur National Monument is to be sacrificed to Reclamation," Chapman's predecessor, Harold Ickes, wrote to columnist and historian Bernard DeVoto at *Harper's Weekly*, "why not the Yellowstone and other National Parks and Monuments? As you apprehend, it is an entering wedge. Having established such a precedent, Chapman will be besieged for other concessions. I am against them all."

DeVoto did not need to be persuaded. Earlier, he had come to the defense of the entire public lands system when proposals to transfer all federal lands to the states had been offered up in Congress. "The public lands," he wrote in the January 1947 issue of *Harper's Weekly*,

> are first to be transferred to the states on the fully justified assumption that if there should be a state government not wholly compliant to the desires of stockgrowers, it could be pressured into compliance. . . . From the states the public lands are to be transferred to private ownership. Present holders of permits [for grazing on public lands] are to be constituted a prior and privileged caste. . . . They are to be permitted to buy the lands—the public lands, the West's lands, your lands—at a fraction of what they are worth. And the larger intention is to liquidate all the publicly held resources of the West.

Outbursts like that had been instrumental in defeating the attempted raid in 1948, and DeVoto applied the same energy to the Dinosaur fight, getting a platoon of writers, including Joseph Wood Krutch and Wallace Stegner, to join him in submitting polemics against the Dinosaur dams for publication in everything from the *Atlantic* to the *Saturday Review of Literature*. The fact that the Bureau of Reclamation had "picked the two sites within the monument, and plugged for them," Stegner wrote with dark (and fully justified) suspicion in the February 15, 1954, issue of the *New Republic*, "suggests that perhaps it *wants* to infringe the sanctity of the parks. . . . It could build dams with much freer hand and have to compromise less with other interests if it could break down the national park immunity. Something similar might be guessed of Secretary McKay [Chapman's successor at Interior]; one who ponders the evidence might well conclude not only that Secretary McKay is willing to violate park territory, but he would like nothing better."

The conservation community, just beginning to react to the ethic of unbridled growth that would characterize the postwar years, added its own small but increasingly vigorous contributions to the effort. Howard Zahniser of the Wilderness Society and David Brower of the Sierra Club organized a National Conservation Committee to flood Congress with arguments against the dams. Brower commissioned a four-color film showing what treasures would vanish if the dams were approved and persuaded Stegner to edit and contribute to a book of text and photographs called *This Is Dinosaur*, published at breakneck speed and distributed free of charge by publisher Alfred A. Knopf (who also contributed a chapter). Brower stood up before a congressional committee and studiously pointed out repeated errors in the Bureau of Reclamation's estimates regarding evaporation loss and other arcane hydrological matters, while the Sierra Club put forth alternative sites, including Glen Canyon on the Colorado. And the conservationists won. When the Upper Colorado River Basin Project was approved in 1956, it included language stipulating that no national park or monument could be materially affected by the construction of any dams. Instead, Glen Canyon was chosen as the site for a single, albeit enormous dam.

Ironically, of course, the Sierra Club came to regret having suggested the site, for when Glen Canyon Dam was completed in 1965, one of the most beautiful of all the Colorado's canyon systems vanished beneath the indigo depths of Lake Powell. Neither Brower nor most other conservationists of the time had fully comprehended the loveliness that was at stake, and in 1963, even as the reservoir's waters were beginning to snake into the canyon's lower recesses, a remorseful Brower gave Glen Canyon a kind of obituary by publishing an "Exhibit Format" book, *The Place No One Knew: Glen Canyon on the Colorado River*. Featuring eighty luminous color photographs of the canyon by Eliot Porter, the book would, Brower hoped, "be as ageless as the canyon should have been."

The Dinosaur fight had two additional—and much less unhappy—side effects. First, it gave the conservation community an almost unprecedented sense of common mission that made the fate of Dinosaur National Monument an issue of national interest because it was able to tap into and happily exploit a postwar population whose greater individual wealth, greater leisure, greater mobility, and profoundly enlarged understanding and appreciation of natural beauty would help to make environmentalism one of the major social movements of our time. Second, the fight made it clear to many preservation advocates that, in spite of a more supportive public, unless things changed the protection of such fragile places as the wild country of Dinosaur National Monument would be a matter of desperately mounting one exhausting battle after another as one place after another came under assault from those who would use it and use it up for transient commercial ends. What the movement needed was a law that would make it possible to designate wilderness areas that would be protected forever—not merely in the national parks and monuments, as Harold Ickes had wanted in 1939, but throughout the nearly 650 million acres of the entire federal lands system.

So it was that only a few weeks after the Dinosaur victory in 1956, the Wilderness Society's Howard Zahniser drafted the first version of a Wilderness Act establishing a National Wilderness Preservation System and had it introduced in Congress by Senator Hubert Horatio Humphrey of Minnesota. Eight years later, after no fewer than sixty-six revisions, most of them penned in by Zahniser himself, and, in spite of opposition from many of the same people—or at least many of the same *kinds* of people—who had risen up against the Ickes wilderness proposal of 1939, the Wilderness Act of 1964 was passed by both houses of Congress and signed into law by President Lyndon B. Johnson. "In order to assure that an increasing population, accompanied by expanding settlement and growing mechanization, does not occupy and modify all areas within the United States and its possessions, leaving no lands designated for preservation and protection in their natural condition," the act's preamble stated, "it is hereby declared to be the policy of the Congress to secure for the American people of present and future generations the benefits of an enduring resource of wilderness." A wilderness, as the act defined it, was a place "untrammeled by man, where man is a visitor who does not remain," and therefore would be kept forever free of roads, vehicles, commercial development, formal campsites, or any other significant mark of modern human presence.

By the middle of the 1990s, after thirty years of state-by-state wilderness battles, the National Wilderness Preservation System had grown to more than 104 million acres. Most of these protected areas, however, were still confined to national park, national forest, and national wildlife refuge lands, for one of the compromises that had assured passage of the Wilderness Act was that the nearly 300 million acres of lands administered by the Bureau of Land Management would be left out of the wilderness equation, at least for the moment. The BLM, a utilitarian-minded agency cobbled together out of the old General

Land Office and the Grazing Service in 1946, was largely dedicated to grazing, mining, and other commercial uses of its land. It had little interest in wilderness either as idea or as act, and most western congressmen and senators were entirely in sympathy with that tradition. It was not until passage of the Federal Land Policy and Management Act of 1976—the "organic" act designed to coordinate the administration of the nation's public lands outside those already designated as parks, forests, or wildlife refuges—that the agency had been ordered to begin studying its lands to see which areas could be recommended for addition to the National Wilderness Preservation System.

The BLM, dubbed the "Bureau of Livestock and Mining" by sarcastic environmentalists, met its wilderness assignment with a kind of surly institutional resentment that caused it to overlook or disqualify many areas that a more objective investigation would have found to be entirely appropriate as additions to the system. Congress, whose public land committees remained largely dominated by western members, was slow to act on even those recommendations that the BLM was willing to submit, and by the middle of the 1990s, only California and Arizona had been graced with significant designations of BLM wilderness, while such states as Oregon, Colorado, Washington, Wyoming, Montana, Nevada, and New Mexico remained uncorrupted by such preservation.

In no state was the BLM more reluctant to make recommendations or its congressional delegation less willing to support any wilderness designations than Utah. It was not until 1986 that the BLM was ready to announce its recommendations for lands that should be added to the National Wilderness Preservation System. Out of a total of 22 million acres of unappropriated public land in the state, it had managed to discover only 3.2 million acres of Wilderness Study Areas (WSAs) worthy of investigation—the last 600,000 acres of which had been added only after conservationists had filed appeals with the Interior Board of Land Appeals. Out of these 3.2 million, the agency's investigators found only 1.9 million acres that it recommended be designated wilderness. This would not do, declared the Utah Wilderness Coalition. An agglomeration of more than thirty national and regional conservation organizations, ranging from the Sierra Club and the Wilderness Society to the Grand Canyon Trust and led by the particularly feisty Southern Utah Wilderness Alliance, the UWC promptly called for volunteers and launched its own inventory of potential wilderness, publishing the results in 1990 in *Wilderness at the Edge: A Citizen Proposal to Protect Utah's Canyons and Deserts.*

Here were at least 5.7 million acres that clearly qualified for designation, the UWC survey said, some in the West Desert region between central Utah and Nevada, but most in the southern part of the state. Here were the canyons of the Dirty Devil River east of the Henry Mountains, for example, 175,300 acres of twisting mazes and side-canyons whose layer-cake colors and complexity rivaled those of the Grand Canyon itself. How could the BLM decide that only a pittance of this was worth saving? For that matter, how could it leave out of consideration most of the land surrounding Labyrinth Canyon on the Green River as it curled through several hundred million years of redrock geology on its way to meet the Colorado? The UWC found 120,000 acres worth saving there, the BLM only 20,500. The looming eminence of Factory Butte near Hanksville seemed like a good thing to preserve, the conservationists decided, though the BLM apparently had found it dull and worthless. And what about the Anasazi ruins tucked into the walls and alcoves of Arch Canyon in the extreme southeastern corner of the state above Comb Ridge, or the tangled riparian habitat of the Escalante River as it slid past tow-

THE PROBLEM

ering walls of slickrock east of the Kaiparowits Plateau? Indeed, what *about* the 650,000 acres of Kaiparowits Plateau wilderness? Were they dispensable? The BLM thought most of them were. The UWC didn't.

And so it went, from Thompson Canyon in the Book Cliffs to Muddy Creek in the San Rafael Swell: everywhere, the citizen survey consistently found more wilderness worth the saving than did the BLM. Having found it, the UWC went about the business of trying to preserve it with wilderness legislation, a campaign that began in 1989 with H.R. 1500, a bill calling for 5.1 million acres of wilderness and introduced and promoted vigorously, if vainly, by Utah congressman Wayne Owens, who managed to gain 100 cosponsors before he left Congress after an unsuccessful bid for a Senate seat. After that, new information expanded the UWC's proposed wilderness acreage to the 5.7 million outlined in *Wilderness at the Edge*, and the campaign centered around Representative Maurice Hinchey's (D-N.Y.) 1993 Redrock Wilderness Act. While it, too, slowly gathered cosponsors in the House, and while SUWA, the Wilderness Society, and other members of the UWC kept up an increasingly effective drumroll of media publicity, Hinchey's bill remained mired in a legislative bog. Much of Congress, as well as the public, appeared indifferent to the cause of Utah wilderness.

Then the opponents of wilderness, succumbing to an attack of old-fashioned hubris, did something wonderfully stupid. A new age had now begun, the antienvironmentalists of the 104th Congress said upon sliding into their seats on January 4, 1995. The extremist lunatics who had been setting the environmental agenda for this country for too many years, they claimed, would finally be stifled and their misguided attempts to strangle progress rejected. Among these uncaped crusaders was Utah representative Jim Hansen, a veteran antiwilderness champion and new chairman of the House Subcommittee on National Parks, Forests, and Lands. Supported by Utah senators Orrin Hatch and Bob Bennett, Hansen decided to take care of the vexatious "wilderness problem" once and for all by getting a minimalist wilderness bill introduced and passed while the Republican domination of the new Congress was in full swing. The Utah delegation was joined in this desire by Utah governor Mike Leavitt, who proposed that the sixteen wilderness-rich counties in the southern and western parts of the state be encouraged to hold public hearings to determine how much of that wilderness their citizens might want designated. Most of the rest of the state's twenty-nine counties were urban and not invited to participate—for fear, some skeptics believed, that their citizens would want too much wilderness in the state, while officials in the rural counties could be trusted to be parsimonious at best.

If so, that confidence was not misplaced. In Garfield County, for example, where the wilderness hearings were chaired by county commissioner Louise Liston—who believed that the National Wilderness Preservation System was mainly "a hide-away for sex and drugs"—the public notice announcing the first of the hearings left little doubt in anyone's mind about the desired results: "We feel very strongly that lands that do not fit the 1964 Wilderness Bill criteria should not be designated as wilderness, and we need your help in documenting proof as to why we are not including them." On April 1, the governor's office released the results of the three-month hearing process: a total of only 994,414 acres of wilderness recommended by the counties, a figure that did not surprise anyone, though it appalled many. Leavitt then announced that regional hearings would be held in Cedar City, Moab, Salt Lake City, and other cities around the state to gauge reaction to the proposals offered up by the counties.

If most of the county hearings had been generally peaceful affairs, often so heavily stacked in favor of the antiwilderness crowd as to render the prowilderness gang both speechless and all but invisible, the regional hearings, during which wilderness advocates made themselves heard in more than respectable numbers, demonstrated that preservationist sentiment ran a good deal stronger in Utah than its congressional delegation and its governor might have suspected. This was made abundantly clear during the Salt Lake City hearing on April 15, when hundreds of people crowded into the University of Utah's cavernous Orson Spencer Hall. "Every seat is filled," Ray Wheeler wrote in a report on the day for *High Country News.* "More than a hundred people stand or sit in the aisles; another hundred jam into the foyer, where students perch like roosting birds atop rows of cabinets. Fifty more people mill in the lobby outside the auditorium, where a harried official sits at a table surrounded by would-be speakers demanding to know why their names cannot be found on the speaker list. In all, somewhere between 700 and 1,000 Utahns will visit the auditorium during today's four-hour public hearing on BLM wilderness. One in ten will have an opportunity to speak."

They had a lot to say in the two minutes allotted to each of them, those one in ten, and most of it was in favor of more rather than less wilderness. Few were more eloquent than Ann Martin, a recovering victim of cancer, who directed her remarks at Governor Leavitt.

I thought fighting a personal battle against a breast cancer diagnosis was hard, but this wilderness battle is perhaps as hard. Because without these lands and our commitment to protect them, the beauty goes out of this life. . . . The land gives us balance, adds to our spirituality, and reminds us that we are not barbarians after all. . . . Governor . . . as you are able to visit these areas, look at them, please walk in them a bit, look at the black ridged cryptobiotic soils, the seeps and ancient dwellings—listen to the massive rocks and contemplate a Utah, an America, or a world without them.

Cindy King, vice-chairwoman of the Tooele chapter of the Sierra Club, chose to stand in silence in order to "demonstrate what this process is trying to do to the public," and as she stood, a mounting wave of applause rolled through the crowded auditorium, while a chant of "5.7 ... 5.7 ... 5.7" became so loud that it rendered useless the gavel of the hearing's moderator, Utah representative Enid Waldholz.

On June 1, Hansen introduced into the House H.R. 1745, the Utah Public Lands Act of 1995, a bill soon matched in the Senate by S.R. 884, sired by Hatch and Bennett. Both bills led to charges that the entire wilderness review process had been a cynical sham. "The process was designed to put as much information as possible into the hands of the people who make the decisions," environmental consultant Brooke Williams, who had helped monitor the review for the governor's office, complained to a reporter. "But I don't see how they used it. I'm convinced they would have come up with the same conclusion if they hadn't gone through the process." The two bills called for only 1.8 million acres of wilderness, and while that figure looked generous when compared to the county proposal of less than a million acres, it was still smaller than even the miserly BLM recommendation of 1986.

Just as bad, from the environmentalist point of view, the bills included "hard release" language stipulating that other BLM lands in Utah "shall not be managed for the purpose of protecting their suitability for wilderness designation," thereby eviscerating the entire WSA system and obviating the possibility that any other BLM lands in the state could ever be designated as wilderness. Finally, the bills included numerous exceptions to the Wilderness Act of 1964 that environmentalists feared would have allowed pipelines, roads, and even dams and reservoirs to be constructed in some of the designated wilderness.

Predictably, the results infuriated the members of the Utah Wilderness Coalition. "This wasn't a wilderness designation process," said Pamela Eaton, director of the Wilderness Society's Four Corners office in Denver. "It was a wilderness elimination process." Just so, SUWA executive director Mike Matz remembered a year later. "They pulled together the absolutely worst wilderness bill that has ever been assembled," he told me as we sat on the edge of the ridge overlooking Calf Creek Falls in the Escalante drainage. "Not only did their bill designate a paltry amount of wilderness in this vast landscape, it went after the meaning of wilderness itself. They wanted to change it." That act of hubris, Matz said, was their downfall. "It helped us rally people around the country who care about wilderness and want to see that concept preserved. The delegation overreached and bit off more than it could chew."

The bill was so bad that not even the BLM could support it. "It is the position of the BLM," Robert Armstrong, assistant secretary of the Interior for Lands, Minerals, and Management, wrote to New Jersey senator Bill Bradley, "that far too little land is protected under this bill and too much land is released for development. In short, no one should be claiming the support of the Bureau of Land Management and its professional staff." Encouraged by local sentiment and almost certainly cheered by the BLM's apparent change of heart (at least in the agency's Washington offices), wilderness advocates appeared in force at committee field hearings conducted by Hansen in Cedar City and Salt Lake City in June, and at hearings in Washington, D.C., in July, though few were asked to testify.

National environmental groups sent out direct mail pieces, alerting some 150,000 citizens to the dangers of the proposal. Brant

Calkin, a former executive director of SUWA, went on the road to 120 cities in twenty-four states in a VW van, offering a dual-projector slide show that illuminated all the glory that the Utah delegation would leave open to development. Actor and longtime Utah resident Robert Redford, who rations his public appearances carefully, not only made himself available to reporters to discuss his support of Utah wilderness but also traveled to Washington and met with senators. Salt Lake City writer and naturalist Terry Tempest Williams joined with photographer-writer Stephen Trimble, also of Salt Lake, to send a round-robin letter to writers throughout the West, asking that they contribute to a compilation of remarks supporting the wilderness idea in Utah and opposing the Hansen-Hatch-Bennett bills.

The response was immediate, and in September the collection was privately printed and published as *Testimony: Writers of the West Speak on Behalf of Utah Wilderness* (it would be reprinted a year later in a more formal incarnation by Milkweed Editions), then presented to Congress and the media at a press conference in Washington, D.C. Contributors ranged from National Book Award winner Barry Lopez and Pulitzer Prize winner N. Scott Momaday to former Poet Laureate Mark Strand and nationally known journalist John McPhee; together their comments demonstrated both the depth and the breadth of concern for the wild places of Utah. The significance of these areas, Montana essayist and short story writer Rick Bass wrote, goes beyond what they hold for us of economic, scenic, biological, or even spiritual values, however important all of these are; these wild places, he said, are part of the natural inheritance that helps to define us as a people:

> To hold on to one of the last things truly American, and truly unique—a sense of place in the American West—would be an act of strength and a continued source of great power: not the West

of the Marlboro Man and Chevrolet commercials, but the creative, healthy, and untouched West: the sage and pinyon, the rock and sand, the small burrowing owls, the herons. The glitter of stars on a clear small pool of water. The print of deer or lion in the sand, in touched country, as you sleep—it is these things that allow you, allow us, to continue being American, rather than something-else, anything-else, everything-else.

The response of the literary environmentalists to the Hatch-Hansen-Bennett bills might have been expected; that of the nation's press was a little more startling. The *New York Times* was angered by the proposal. So were the *St. Louis Post-Dispatch*, the *Washington Post*, the *Los Angeles Times*, the *Trenton (N.J.) Times*, the *Tampa Tribune*, the *San Francisco Chronicle*, the *Denver Post*, and many, many other newspapers that editorialized against the bills. "You don't have to be a save-the-snail-darter environmentalist," *USA Today* wrote of Hansen's legislation, "to recognize this bill as a real stinker." In Missouri, the *Kansas City Star* agreed, saying that "Congress needs to stop this destructive proposal dead in its tracks." In Iowa, the *Des Moines Register* thought it was "ironic that the congressional delegation closest to the beauty of southern Utah should be so eager to destroy it," while in Maine, the *Portland Press Herald*, calling the exceptions to the Wilderness Act "a horrible precedent," warned that if "the Utah congressional delegation succeeds in putting a bullet in the head of future wilderness in that state, the report from the pistol shot will be heard in Maine. Not only the red rock wilderness of that desert state would be in peril, but so would the Caribou-Speckled Mountain Wilderness of the Pine Tree State." And in Utah, where more than 70 percent of the calls, letters, and petitions received by the governor's Office of Planning and Budget in June supported 5.7 million acres of wilderness, even the resoundingly conservative *Salt Lake City Tribune* told the state's congressional delegation that it should return to Washington "with a clear charge: The bill needs work."

Utah wilderness was no longer just a local issue to be growled over by a handful of environmentalists and a clot of local antiwilderness advocates in league with corporate interests. Like the Dinosaur fight of the 1950s, it was national news now, and the support for wilderness that erupted when the flaws in the bad bills were exposed was broad enough to encourage open opposition even in Congress. In the House, Hansen pulled H.R. 1745 before risking a vote. In the Senate, when Hatch and Bennett tacked S.R. 884 to an Omnibus Parks and Recreation Act in March 1996, Senator Bill Bradley (D-N.J.) filibustered against it. "I know that some of my colleagues will argue that preservation of Utah's unique natural heritage is a matter best left to the State's own delegation with its considerable wisdom and considerable talent," Bradley said with wry diplomacy during his marathon speech. "In this case, I have to disagree. Wilderness is a gift we give to our children and grandchildren, a gift that once destroyed can never be reconstructed. The children of New Jersey deserve it, as much as the children of California or Colorado. . . . Mr. President, this is about time and silence, and the chance for future generations to explore and understand this vast and beautiful wilderness." In the end, Bradley got enough support to kill the whole parks bill (though it was later passed without the Utah amendment). The environmentalists had won a battle. But not the war.

THE DEFEAT OF THE "antiwilderness" bill of 1996 was worthy of celebration, but the prowilderness crowd did not take to dancing in the streets. There was too much to worry about. Chief among such worries was the little-known Kaiparowits Plateau. Here, while the Utah

Wilderness Coalition and the Utah state delegation were locked in combat over wilderness proposals, Conoco Oil had petitioned the Interior Department for permission to explore for oil and gas and to develop any promising finds. Even more troubling, the area was threatened by a proposed twenty-five-thousand-acre underground coal mine to be operated by a Dutch-controlled outfit called Andalex Resources. "The Andalex proposal," SUWA's issues director Ken Rait warned the members of his organization in its quarterly newsletter,

> entails a 22-mile paved highway where none exists today and powerlines constructed along an entirely separate corridor across proposed wilderness. Their plan calls for mine vents, ancillary roads, communications facilities, and a host of other mine-related infrastructure sprawled over five areas proposed for wilderness designation by the Utah Wilderness Coalition: Nipple Bench, Squaw Canyon, Wahweap/Coyote Creek, Burning Hills, and Warm Creek. The Andalex coal mine would irreversibly impact half the units proposed for wilderness designation in the Kaiparowits region.

If the project were approved by the Interior Department, he said, the mined coal would be carried across the plateau on newly built roads to railheads on 130,000-pound forty-two-wheelers—one truck every eight minutes, twenty-four hours a day, for forty years, one estimate had it—then sent by rail to Long Beach, California, for eventual shipment to markets in Japan, Korea, and Taiwan.

The proposal was supported by Hatch, Bennett, and Hansen and the usual clutch of local entrepreneurs, particularly those in Kanab, the seat of Kane County, where the prospect of getting as many as nine hundred jobs out of the project glimmered like a heat mirage hovering over the sagebrush-dotted flats and slickrock canyons of the

Kaiparowits. But in the little town of Boulder on the other side of the plateau, one environmentalist resident succinctly predicted a battle of potentially epic proportions, something to compare with that over old-growth forests in the Pacific Northwest, where people were still being hauled off to jail for attempting to block timber sales. "Over my dead body," he told me grimly. "Whatever it takes, that ain't going in. End of story."

That story indeed ended—though somewhat differently than anyone might have expected. The Andalex mine proposal was thwarted (at least for what was hoped would be a good long time)—not because wild-haired environmentalists chained themselves to bulldozers or blocked access roads with their bodies or otherwise put their lives and fortunes in the way of development, or even because the corporate entities involved thought better of their development plans. A presidential Executive Order was the weapon that did the project in. On September 25, 1996, President Bill Clinton, acting on the seed of an idea planted in the White House by redrock enthusiasts months before, validated the proposal first offered by the Interior Department under Harold L. Ickes in 1939: At a speech on the North Rim of the Grand Canyon, surrounded by supporters of Utah wilderness, including Robert Redford and Terry Tempest Williams, and with the old curmudgeon's second son, Harold, in attendance as his deputy chief of staff, Clinton cited that earlier effort and then announced that he had just invoked the Antiquities Act of 1906 to establish the 1.7-million-acre Grand Staircase–Escalante National Monument, a new conservation unit that would include not only the unprotected canyons of the Escalante River and its tributaries but all of the Kaiparowits, including 650,000 acres of proposed wilderness.

Reaction from many politicians and county officials in Utah could have been borrowed whole from outbursts that had erupted after several such presidential acts in the past—as when President Theodore Roosevelt had offended copper-mining interests by using the Antiquities Act to establish Grand Canyon National Monument in 1908, for example; or when Franklin Roosevelt had inspired the wrath of the livestock industry when he invoked the act to create a national monument in Jackson Hole, Wyoming, in 1943; or—most dramatically—when Jimmy Carter had incurred the rage of timber, mining, and oil interests in 1978 by setting aside fifty-six million acres of land in Alaska as national monuments until they could be protected under the terms of the Alaska National Interest Lands Conservation Act in 1980.

That all these interim measures ultimately resulted in the addition of millions of acres of land owned by all Americans to now-cherished national park and national wildlife refuge systems and that states, counties, and local communities still continued to derive great economic benefit from them was a fact ignored by the Utah congressional delegation, which responded with well-worn cries of "land grab," as well as by local spokesmen such as Kane County Attorney Colin Winchester. "We have had it up to here with the federal government," Winchester said, echoing a couple of decades of "Sagebrush Rebellion" and "Wise Use" rhetoric. "The people born and raised down here feel they know how to handle this land better than people in Washington, or in the Wasatch Front." In Escalante, President Clinton and Interior Secretary Bruce Babbitt were hanged in effigy, and, in Kanab, county officials held their own press conference to coincide with the president's event at the Grand Canyon, releasing funeral-black balloons under signs reading, "Shame on You, Clinton."

For its part, the environmental community reacted with what

might best be described as cautious glee. "It was kind of overwhelming," said SUWA's Mike Matz, who attended the Grand Canyon announcement. "There you are, standing in an incredible spot, and the president of the United States is announcing the establishment of a new national monument. It was pretty emotional." After all, he went on, "just two years before that a new Congress had come in and we were all worried about what was going to happen, and for events to have changed like that in the face of such a hostile political climate was thrilling." Matz also dismissed complaints that Clinton's act was just election-year politics. "What isn't political, these days?" he asked me when I brought the subject up. "That's how you get things done. It's all politics. It's getting enough people educated on the issues, getting them concerned enough to make their concerns known to their elected officials—that's what makes this country work."

At the same time, Matz, like many others, had some concerns about the new monument. For one thing, he noted, there still were 1.3 million acres in the Escalante and Kaiparowits segments of the monument that awaited designation as wilderness, a goal that should not be lost in the glow of celebration—nor should the overall goal of 5.7 million acres of Utah wilderness be forgotten, he said. For another, the BLM—which the president's order stipulated would remain the agency in charge of the new monument (the National Park Service administers most)—would have to be watched carefully to be certain that the natural, archeological, and paleontological resources of the area were managed properly. "We're going to have to participate extensively in the development of the management plan for the monument over the next three years," he said, "to ensure that there aren't a whole slew of visitor facilities put in, to ensure that stretches like the Hole-in-the-Rock Road or the Cottonwood Wash Road aren't paved, and that there aren't a lot of developed campsites around. We don't want to make this area like a lot of national parks, which are just magnets for people in RVs and whatnot. It would be nice to have another large chunk of land set aside that should be managed essentially as wilderness—like Kings Canyon National Park in California or the Everglades in Florida."

Given the backlog of contested actions that the various district offices of the BLM had initiated or approved in many proposed wilderness areas over the previous several years (though not always getting its way), the concern did not seem unwarranted. These included the "chaining" of piñon pine and juniper in such places as the Henry Mountains—destroying hundreds of thousands of acres of these ancient "P-J" forests just as completely as the Forest Service's more publicized clear-cutting in the Pacific Northwest had obliterated old-growth Douglas fir—as well as persistent overgrazing, threatened oil drilling, proposed dams and reservoirs, military overflights and missile target runs, and the invasion of armies of filmmaking crews.

The environmentalist concern was aggravated by fear of local actions, too, particularly those of county officials. Citing a vaguely understood 1866 federal law, Revised Statute 2477 (since rescinded), which provides that the builder of a road on nonreserved federal land effectively owns the right of way, those officials had acquired the ugly habit of bulldozing roads into wilderness study areas along what they claimed were old established state roads—though, in truth, usually along tracks so old and infrequently used as to barely qualify as game trails, much less as "established" roads, and in many cases where no roads of any kind had in fact ever existed. Whether they claimed a legal right or were simply venting their spleens via bulldozer, their motives were clear enough, at least according to Ken Sleight, proprietor of the Pack Creek Ranch resort outside Moab: "They want to blade these roads so they can assure that there will never be wilderness," he complained to a reporter for *High Country News.* "It's tragic, but that's the way it is. They're ticked off about wilderness and the president's establishment of Grand Staircase–Escalante National Monument."

Indeed, not long after President Clinton's designation of the new monument, Kane County officials rammed three such roads into the Moquith Mountain, Burning Hills, and Paria-Hackberry Wilderness Study Areas. Officials in Garfield County went Kane County one better, bulldozing four roads into Grand Staircase–Escalante National Monument itself, including the Devil's Garden Wilderness Study Area, while those in San Juan County ignored a restraining order obtained by the BLM and bulldozed 10.7 miles of road into the proposed wilderness of Harts Point near Canyonlands National Park. "Until a judge tells us they're not our roads," San Juan County commissioner Bill Redd boasted, "we're going to continue. Just because someone doesn't like it doesn't mean he can tell me to quit." And until the federal government was willing to prosecute such violations with determination, environmentalists worried, potential wilderness in the monument and elsewhere would remain at risk.

For a while, however, they were just as worried about the risks the government itself seemed willing to take. At the same time that the president made his announcement, the BLM approved Conoco's plan to do some exploratory drilling for oil and gas on state-owned land in the heart of the new monument. The government, environmentalists charged, was playing dice with the future of the plateau, gambling that the company would not find a commercially valid deposit and ultimately would lose interest even in the claims it had applied for on federal lands in the region. Perhaps; but in time the government's decision began to look like a reasonably wise move. First, early in 1998 the Interior Department hedged its bets by negotiating a land exchange with the state government that gave the federal government title not only to all state-owned lands in the monument but to all state-controlled oil and coal leases as well. Congressional legislation to approve the deal was introduced in the spring by none other than Jim Hansen. Second, the BLM superseded Conoco's oil lease applications until the company decided whether it would be worthwhile going ahead with them. Finally, and most important, Conoco came up dry—or nearly so—with its exploratory well. By the summer of 1998, the Kaiparowits no longer looked like much of an opportunity for the company, and it never did pursue its federal lease applications. The government's gamble, if gamble it was, had paid off.

Which still left the question of wilderness designation, in the monument as elsewhere. "We will never quit until we pass our wilderness bill," Senator Orrin Hatch had insisted after Bradley's 1996 filibuster victory in the Senate. "It may take another Congress, but we will never quit." Perhaps not, but another wrench was soon thrown into the antiwilderness machinery. At a House Resources Committee hearing on April 24, 1996, Jim Hansen had challenged Interior Secretary Bruce Babbitt to prove his claim, based on the UWC inventory, that at least five million acres of BLM land in Utah did in fact qualify as wilderness. Babbitt replied that he would take Hansen's challenge as a suggestion for the BLM to conduct another survey of the lands in question and come back with a more precise wilderness inventory. "I'm ready to begin," he told Hansen, and, not long after Senator Bradley strangled the Hatch-Bennett amendment in its crib, the Interior Department had gotten the new study under way.

The Utah Wilderness Coalition beat the Interior Department to the punch. Not long after Babbitt's announcement, the UWS decided to do another citizen survey of its own. The first time around, limited resources—human and monetary—had prevented volunteers from taking a comprehensive look at places like the West Desert region in the west central part of the state. They hoped to expand the original proposal, but also feared that some areas in the original survey would have been so damaged by roading or other development that they would no longer qualify as designated wilderness. Beginning in the summer of 1996, platoons of volunteers—some three hundred people would be involved before the survey was done—set off into the mountains, plateaus, mesas, and canyons of wild Utah armed with cameras, compasses, topographical maps, and global-positioning-system receivers. Sure enough, after forty thousand aerial and on-the-ground photographs and fifty-five thousand hours of exploration, the coalition announced in July 1998 that it would in fact have to drop some wilderness sites from its original proposal. Still, the coalition was happy to report, about 99 percent of its previous inventory still met wilderness standards. "This is a testament to the quality of the original inventory and to years of hard work defending Utah's unprotected de facto wilderness," it said.

Now, the coalition went on, for the *really* good news: more than 3 million acres of new de facto wilderness had been discovered—including 20,000 acres of riparian habitat along Willow Creek in the Book Cliffs region, some 50,000 acres of mesas and gorges and redrock walls in the Lockhart Basin of the Canyonlands Basin, more than 225,000 acres in four new proposed wilderness units in the San Rafael Swell, and dozens of other additions scattered from Grand Staircase National Monument to the Great Basin. The new demand would be for 9.1 million acres of Utah wilderness, and a whole new fight was under way—complicated in the summer of 1998 when Congressman Hansen introduced legislation that would open up much of the San Rafael Swell to development.

THE PROBLEM

Hansen's bill languished, stalled, like virtually everything else in Congress, by the impeachment proceedings against President Clinton. Meanwhile, the BLM issued its draft management plan for the 1.7 million acres of Grand Staircase–Escalante National Monument in early November 1998. In many respects, it was a revolutionary document—at least when compared to the BLM's traditional antipathy toward preservation. Earlier that year, I had asked Kate Cannon, the monument's on-the-ground administrator, if the planning team had encountered major pressure to pave roads and otherwise develop the monument. "No," she said. "That's been one of the interesting surprises. One of the things we heard loud and clear from all constituencies was 'Leave it alone. Keep it remote, keep it rough, keep it difficult to access.' And that's what we intend to do."

Just as Cannon had promised, the draft plan's "preferred alternative" for management was long on wilderness and short on development. The emphasis throughout was on the natural and scientific values of the monument. More than a million acres would be managed as "primitive" zones, with access and use restricted to preserve their wilderness characteristics. Another half-million acres would be managed as "outback," with their own, somewhat less rigid restrictions. There would be no paved roads anywhere in the monument, no RV hookups, no big parking lots, no concessions. All tourist and administrative facilities would be built in surrounding communities—the biggest in Escalante—giving each town an economic stake in the monument's preservation and going a long way toward diluting old angers.

The plan did meet with mixed feelings from some quarters. "I'm concerned," Louise Liston told me, "that it's clearly slanted toward preservation, and I worry that some historic uses of the land will be restricted." At the same time, she said, she favored the emphasis on the educational and scientific importance of the monument. So did Mike Matz, executive director of SUWA. His organization and other wilderness advocates would be advocating that most of the "outback" zones be managed as wilderness, as those in the "primitive" zones would be, until such time as they could be folded into the National Wilderness Preservation System under the terms of the Redrock Wilderness Act. Still, on the whole, he said, he found the plan "a whole lot better than we might have expected."

The Grand Staircase–Escalante plan was one thing; Utah wilderness was another, and that issue was no closer to resolution at the end of 1998 than it had been at any time since the middle of the 1980s.

Clearly, as the fate of Utah's wilderness continues to be debated in the cloakrooms and cubbyholes of Congress, wilderness advocates in and out of Utah have reason to believe that eternal vigilance is the price of preservation. But is ear-biting confrontation forever going to dominate environmental politics in Utah, and is boom-and-bust resource extraction going to spell an end to both wilderness and the hope of a sustainable life in canyon country? I think maybe not, in spite of all the noise that still attends wilderness discussions. If I am right, it will be because so many people in southern Utah seem to be asking these kinds of questions of themselves and one another for the first time.

Trail to Phipps–Death Hollow, in the proposed Escalante Canyons
Wilderness, in Grand Staircase–Escalante National Monument (1989)

San Rafael River canyons from the Wedge, in the proposed San Rafael Swell
Wilderness (1989)

Opposite Along the Paria River, in the proposed Kaiparowits Plateau
Wilderness, in Grand Staircase–Escalante National Monument (1998)

Storm over Tarantula Mesa, in the proposed Henry Mountains Wilderness.
The view is from Strike Valley Overlook, in Capitol Reef National Park.
Oystershell Reef is directly below (1988).

Mudstone formations on the Paria River, in the proposed Kaiparowits
Plateau Wilderness, in Grand Staircase–Escalante National Monument
(1998)

Desiccated piñon, Arch Canyon, in the proposed San Juan–Anasazi
Wilderness (1992)

Opposite Along the Escalante River, in the proposed Escalante Canyons
Wilderness, in Grand Staircase–Escalante National Monument (1989)

Beaver dam on the Escalante River, in the proposed Escalante Canyons Wilderness, in Grand Staircase–Escalante National Monument (1989)

Upper Calf Creek Falls, in the proposed Escalante Canyons Wilderness, in
Grand Staircase–Escalante National Monument (1993)

Looking toward Tarantula Mesa, in the proposed Henry Mountains
Wilderness (1990)

Wind circles in the sand along the Dirty Devil River, in the proposed Dirty
Devil River Wilderness (1991)

Escalante Arch, in the proposed Escalante Canyons Wilderness, in Grand
Staircase–Escalante National Monument (1989)

Smoky Mountain Road splitting the proposed Kaiparowits Plateau
Wilderness, in Grand Staircase–Escalante National Monument (1998)

CONCLUSION: THE PROSPECT

THE PIANIST LEANED INTO THE MUSIC, urging his fingers along as they negotiated a slow-moving but complicated jazz riff he had just improvised for *As Time Goes By*. He glided through the passage; then, with a sly, satisfied grin, tinkled his way to the end of the song and sent out a final soft note that echoed sweetly in the low-ceilinged room. Diners put down their knives and forks and sent up a round of restrained but indisputably sincere applause.

Though the music was good enough to qualify, the pianist was not sitting in at Bemelmans Bar in the Hotel Carlyle in Manhattan and playing to a crowd of urban jazz aficionados. The pianist was Ed Lueders, a novelist, poet, and retired professor of poetry and literature at the University of Utah and a recent transplant to southern Utah. He was playing at the Capitol Reef Inn, an unpretentious restaurant and motel situated at the western limits of Torrey, Utah. The customers included a few locals, some of them still in their work clothes, but most were tourists.

What brought the tourists to this town, little more than a wide spot on Utah State Highway 24, with big old arching cottonwood trees, dusty side lanes, often rickety domestic architecture, and the occasional horse pasture, was suggested by the mural that offers a slightly abstract view of slickrock wilderness on one wall of the dining room. This, together with the casual blend of generic country kitchen and splashy southwestern motifs that served as decor in the rest of the place, made it clear that you were now in the heart of canyon country, where the redrock meets the road and the ideas of space and beauty take on entirely new dimensions.

"There's a challenge here," Ed told me later, sitting in the dining alcove of the house he and his wife, Deborah, had constructed amid a scatter of piñon and juniper on a flat just beyond the eastern edge of town. "I guess it's because there is so much more land than there is civilization, and so much more natural hazard, as well as beauty. They go hand in hand. The challenge is to adapt to this in a continuing fashion, day to day. That sense of challenge gives something to the character of the families that are rooted here, who have fought their way through winters and wind and blowing sand." Wind, indeed. Squeezed between the long wall of Boulder Mountain and the Aquarius Plateau on one side and the great pyramidlike humps of Thousand Lake Mountain and the rusty red escarpment of Cooks Mesa at the edge of Capitol Reef National Park on the other, the wind takes on speed and power up here on the Torrey Flats, becoming as much a presence as the ancient multicolored sandstones and shales that define the character of the landscape. The wind can madden you with its persistence, but if you let your mind wander down some philosophical paths, you can begin to think of it as the voice of the land itself. Living here even part-time, Ed believes, can do that kind of thing to you.

"There's a spiritual aspect to be found in the landscape," he said, "the kind of discontent-contentedness that is the basis of any true religion—any valid religion. I want to share this with everybody. I think people ought to have it, and here's the place where it can be had. On the other hand," he adds with a rueful chuckle, "I say, like anyone else who has a vested interest, 'Go away. Don't ruin this. Don't change it.'"

And there it is: the paradox that lies at the heart of southern Utah's future.

IT IS TOO LATE, AS Ed Lueders knows all too well, to ask anyone to go away. People have been coming to Utah in growing numbers for years—there were about 17.4 million of them in 1997, the Utah Travel Council estimates—and there is no reason to think they will not continue to come. Many visitors confine themselves to the ski slopes high in the Wasatch Range in the winter or the trout streams of the Uintas or the La Sals in the summer, but year-round the majority of the invaders head for the southern plateaus, where the state's most popular national parks are located—Arches, Canyonlands, Capitol Reef, Bryce Canyon, and Zion—as well as Glen Canyon National Recreation Area, with the unearthly blue of Lake Powell shining at its redrock heart, and a scattering of national monuments like Natural Bridges and Cedar Breaks. And the brand-new Grand Staircase–Escalante National Monument doubtless is getting its share, recording more than 800,000 visits by November 1998.

They come from everywhere. The voices you hear while traipsing through increasingly crowded national parks or even along nominally isolated backcountry trails include all of the American dialects and the inflections of languages from all over the world, though among the foreign tongues German, French, and Japanese tend to predominate. Whatever their languages, most of those you see are tourists, people who collect the sights and move on, never to return. Others, and there are more and more of them (Utah's population growth rate is one of the highest in the nation), have chosen to settle in Utah;

many of these end up, like Ed and Deborah Lueders, living in southern Utah at least part of every year, stretching the population envelopes of St. George, Hurricane, Moab, and half a dozen other towns. Some, like me, are repeat offenders, plain addicts who, while they have neither the means nor the opportunity to settle here, cannot stay away from this country very long before they get an irresistible urge to return.

It was not always so, at least not in the southern half of the state. Fifty years ago, cattle outnumbered Latter-day Saints, and the Saints outnumbered the tourists. No longer. In part, this is attributable to the uranium rush of the 1950s, but most of the area's renown has been ginned up by several decades of artful promotion by the National Park Service, scenery-rich and cash-poor county governments, and the Utah Travel Division, as well as the blossoming work of a growing cadre of writers, photographers, artists, and filmmakers who have discovered elements of beauty and mystery in canyon country that they find compelling—and, not always coincidentally, eminently marketable.

What they are selling, more often than not, is wilderness—though Utah officialdom usually avoids the word itself for fear of appearing radical. Not just the wild country of the national parks, which remains a staple of the calendar and postcard and coffee-table book trade, but that found in those millions of acres of proposed wilderness whose fate has become a matter of national concern—contributing to the area's repute and exacerbating the confused stew of hope and dismay that haunts many of those who have tried to make a life here. Indeed, it could be argued that the continuing fight over how much federal land should be designated as wilderness, particularly the attempt (however spurious) to get every citizen involved in the discussion through public hearings, may in its own way have been an agent of change almost as significant as the pressures of population growth and tourism. If nothing else, it may have kicked in the beginnings of dialogue and helped get the citizens of southern Utah thinking about the future of their region more seriously than ever before.

As I have noted, some of the ersatz wilderness hearings of 1995 were noisy affairs, with much waving of placards and the kind of angry rhetoric that glows in the dark. On the surface, then, the fight would seem to have given even more ammunition to those (particularly in the national media, ever in search of sound-bite wisdom) who favor a simpleminded depiction of the region as one locked in a virulent clash between environmentalists, usually presented as well-meaning but naive urban elitists, many of them latecomers insensitive to rural values, and the sturdy descendants of local pioneers, whose social and political instincts may be a little primitive but whose struggle to resist change has about it a kind of lonely, misguided heroism. After talking with rancher Dell LeFevre and other locals in Boulder, *Los Angeles Times Magazine* writer Frank Clifford caught the essence of the argument precisely: "None of them is especially fond of the newcomers moving into the rural West—people with soft hands who make a living elsewhere, whose social ties are to New York or Los Angeles," he wrote. "They join environmental groups, pressure Congress to turn grazing land into wilderness preserves and then overrun it with mountain bikes, river rafts, and all-terrain vehicles. . . . You can find a Dell LeFevre cursing into his coffee in virtually every Western crossroads cafe where a mountain view or a desert sunset attracts exiles from the cities."

Both the people and the situation are a good deal more complicated than that. Consider what I saw one evening in the spring of 1995, when I attended a wilderness hearing held by the Grand County Council in Moab's hilltop community center. In the middle of one of the two big adjoining rooms were long tables on which BLM maps had been spread. Other maps were propped up on easels or pinned to the walls. The other room held several dozen auditorium chairs and a couple of tables behind which were arranged the council members. People milled about in the two big rooms under the raw glare of fluorescent lights, poring over maps, huddling in small knots, leaning close to one another in their chairs to talk. Every now and then, a name would be called out and someone would go to a council table, sit down, and attempt to make a case for or against wilderness in Grand County, Utah.

There were the usual collection of environmentalists one would expect to see in southern Utah's little metropolis, together with real estate agents and go-getting local merchants. But among the crowd were a few ranchers who John Wayned up to the council tables in boots caked in mud and flecked with horseshit, wearing limp-brimmed old Stetsons, dirty blue jeans, and work shirts that had seen better days—the uniform of tradition in a region whose oldest citizens could remember when U.S. 160 was the only paved street in town. What I found surprising was not that the ranchers were against wilderness designation, but that they were there at all—not only there, but there to discuss things with outward citizenly calm. It had not been that long, after all, since the days when the very word "wilderness" had been an obscenity that rarely passed the lips of such men, and when Clive Kincaid, the first president of SUWA, had been hung in effigy down in Escalante (often pronounced "Eskalant" in these parts) and other environmentalists allegedly shot at from time to time (warning shots, we can assume; in southern Utah, cowboys tend to hit what they aim at). Yet here they were, talking.

The Moab hearings were not typical, I suppose, and, barring a miraculous turnabout in the United States Congress, it appears certain that the debate over the future of southern Utah's wildlands will continue to bubble fiercely in the months (and maybe years) to come. But, for the first time, much of the nation will be watching the pot while it boils. And thinking about Utah. And thinking maybe it ought to come on down and have a look for itself. Like me, for instance. I returned to canyon country several times between May of 1996 and the fall of 1998. With each trip, I was getting another fix to relieve my addiction to the place, but I was also there to look a little more closely at how things might have changed since I first widened my eyes and heart at the sight of slickrock all those years before, talking to people I had known for years and some I had met only recently, like piano player and poetry professor Ed Lueders in Torrey.

And there was change, considerable change, I found. It seemed to be much on the minds of people in southern Utah—as it is in much of the West. Conflict resolution and coalition building over the question of public land use is a growth industry. Groups of environmentalists, government officials, loggers, ranchers, and even urban boomers and boosters are sitting down together in such places as Missoula, Montana, to talk about grizzly bear recovery; or Ashton, Idaho, to discuss the future of the Henrys Fork watershed; or Montezuma County, Colorado, to outline management policy in San Juan National Forest; or Quincy, California, to hammer out the same for Plumas National Forest.

Reasoning together is not always seen as a universal good; some fear that the development-minded will merely subvert the whole business (as in Utah's wilderness review). "Many community activists like these proposals," the Sierra Club's chairman, Michael McCloskey, wrote in *High Country News*. "They see them as empowering. Many academics praise them, too. And industry likes them"—but for reasons that are all too self-serving, he says. Industries "prefer dealing with community representatives to having to duel with EPA experts at the national level or with representatives of national environmental groups. One company spokesman recently told an audience: 'I don't want bureaucrats telling me how to run my business; I would far prefer to take my chances with people from the community.'" And why shouldn't he? McCloskey asks. "Industry thinks its odds are better in these forums. It believes it can dominate them over time and relieve itself of the burden of tough national rules. It has ways to generate pressures in communities where it is strong, which it doesn't have at the national level."

Even so, in southern Utah many people on both sides of the wilderness question are suddenly aware that the free-wheeling traditions of the past are not going to serve the future very well and that if the quality of life here is going to survive they had better start dealing with change. With the aid of state funding, some towns and all of the counties have been developing master plans; these have been accomplished with varying degrees of effectiveness and commitment (a few have been little more than manifestoes declaring that counties should "take back" "their" land from the federal government and defy all federal regulations), but at least they have been done. And in spite of all the hollering and arm waving over the Utah wilderness bills, most people seem to accept the idea that the coming of wilderness is inevitable, though just how much wilderness Utah's residents are going to either embrace with joy or accept with teeth-grinding resentment remains uncertain. And while the usual clutch of right-wing politicians and ill-tempered local officials continues to bleat about federal arrogance in seizing "Utah's land" for a new national monument, most of those I encountered either were indifferent to President Clinton's action or welcomed it, agreeing with then-congressman Ross C. Anderson. "The view that all Utahns are up in arms because of the designation of this national monument is a horrible misconception," he said. "Most people love this state because of the incredible beauty."

A poll conducted by the *Salt Lake Tribune* in late October of 1996 seemed to validate Anderson's view (though Anderson himself lost his bid for reelection in November). Of the 1,300 Utahns interviewed statewide, about 47 percent said they opposed the monument, 39 percent said they favored it, and 14 percent said they weren't sure. In the region of the monument itself, unsurprisingly, only 34 percent of the respondents said they favored the new park's designation—but, given the area's tradition of ill-tempered resistance to *any* sort of federal reservation, that figure in itself was a major indicator of change. Just as startling was the fact that 44 percent of those interviewed preferred the monument to the proposed coal mine, while only 41 percent would have kept the mine and 15 percent weren't sure.

Most of the people with whom I have talked over the past several years are a good deal less concerned with either wilderness designation or the existence of the new monument than they were with the consequences of unanticipated and uncontrolled growth and a fast-changing economic foundation. Overall in Utah, mining, timber, livestock, and other extractive-industry jobs declined by 5,000 between 1979 and 1993, while nonextractive employment—finance, light industry, state and federal government service, and tourism—grew by 360,000. Tourism, in fact, is now Utah's most important industry, employing an estimated 69,000 people and generating $3.5 *billion* in annual revenue.

What is true for the state in general is true of southern Utah in particular, including the "corridor" of State Highway 12, which curls 114 miles through the mountains and across the plateaus from U.S. 89 just below Panguitch on the west to a juncture with State Highway 24 near Torrey on the east, bringing drivers to the edge of Bryce Canyon National Park and Cedar Breaks National Monument and otherwise carrying them over some of the most spectacular landscape anyone could hope to find (including a good deal of the new national monument), with heartstopping views of Thousand Lake Mountain, Capitol Reef National Park, and the distant blue mass of the Henry Mountains. Until 1986, most of the road had been dirt and gravel and a challenge not to be taken lightly, particularly that portion of it winding over Boulder Mountain between the town of Boulder and Highway 24, the principal access to Capitol Reef National Park from the west. But in 1986 the state paved it, and Highway 12 was now a "Scenic Byway" that could be negotiated by even the most elephantine RV. Every year now, as many as a million vehicles pass over the road, and the corridor stands as a kind of symbol for the choices that now confront much of southern Utah.

At about the same time that the road got paved, the importance of the corridor's traditional industries began to decline. A combination of persistent drought and low prices has put local cattle ranchers dead up against it, in spite of continuing access to federal grazing lands on both BLM lands and Dixie National Forest lands up on Boulder Mountain and other parts of the Aquarius Plateau (at fees, it should be noted, that still fall far below those charged for grazing on private lands). Dell LeFevre, who proudly calls himself a fifth-generation Garfield County native—his family has been farming and ranching here since the 1860s, when his great-great-grandfather became one of Brigham Young's colonizing settlers—is one of those facing an uncertain future. He owns 520 acres near town and leases "about thirty square miles" of federal grazing land on Boulder Mountain, but nevertheless has lost nearly a hundred thousand dollars over the past several years, victimized by drought, by competition from too many wealthy ranchers and ranching corporations who operate at a loss for tax reasons, by the price controls exercised by the four dominant packing houses, and, he insists, by environmental restrictions on how many cows he can run on federal lands. (He also is adamant in his opposition to wilderness designation, though because LeFevre exercises uncommon care in his use of federal land, local wilderness advocate Mark Austin still describes him as "one of the good guys.")

He is not alone in his dilemma, LeFevre told me. "The bottom line is, you got to make a living, and these ranchers are not making it." That is why so many local ranchers are selling their property piecemeal and giving up ranching. The temptation is great, even for him. "I'm 55 years old," he said, "and worth a lot of money, on paper. You take 520 acres in Boulder at $4,000 an acre, and that's a pretty good check. But I don't want that," he added with utter sincerity. "It would tear my heart out. Us old cowboys married this land. If you're a developer and you're trying to turn a fast dollar, land doesn't mean anything to you. It's like trading a car off. But for us old cowboys who have spent our life on this land, it's part of us. I wouldn't be the same Dell LeFevre if I had to sell that land and give up the cattle business."

To avoid that possibility, LeFevre is working with the Colorado Plateau Sustainable Communities Corporation, a group cofounded by Brooke Williams in Salt Lake City and devoted to helping guide local communities in the search for sustainable kinds of economic development. Williams also serves as a consultant to the Sonoran Institute in Tucson, whose "Highway 12 Corridor Project" is designed to find ways for the road's towns, many of which are close to Bryce Canyon or Capitol Reef National Parks, to avoid the social, environmental, and economic strains that industrial tourism and uncontrolled growth often bring to such "gateway" communities.

"What we're doing is identifying five or six or eight projects in these communities that will help them keep at least some of their lifeways," Williams said. With regard to Dell LeFevre and other Boulder ranchers, he added, "We've been talking about how to raise the prices for their cows through a concept called 'Boulder Beef'"—high-quality "natural beef," grown with minimum impact on the land and free of steroids and other chemicals that raise the hackles of pure-food folk—to be marketed to high-end restaurants in Utah and elsewhere. As Williams described it, the idea is not dissimilar to an operation established by entrepreneurs up in Oregon more than twelve years ago, when Patrick "Doc" Hatfield joined with twenty-six other family ranchers to grow and market beef raised according to the principles of "holistic management," a grazing system that ostensibly not only does not damage grassland but also magically improves its condition through carefully controlled rest-and-rotation methods.

The system has plenty of critics, but Hatfield and his fellow ranchers have found that the appeal of "natural" beef is widespread, with restaurants and supermarkets in Washington, Oregon, California, and even Japan now carrying their meat. "The old earth-muffin hippie is blending into the yuppie urban gourmet," Hatfield told a reporter for *Outside* magazine. "They want a little red meat, but they want to know where it's from and how it's produced." Something like the Oregon effort, Williams believes, is going to be necessary to save the open space that the local ranchland represents. "If we're going to be honest," he said, "when we look at those ranches, we have to say, if they aren't raising cows there, they're raising condominiums. They're not going back to nature. I would just as soon have them be cattle ranches as condominiums, myself. So how do we keep those cattle ranches as cattle ranches? By raising the prices they can get for their cows—and maybe Boulder Beef will be the answer to that."

Another good example of an effort to develop a sustainable economic base can be found among small-scale timber operators and lumber mill owners over the mountain in Torrey. Aided again by advice and encouragement from Williams and his group, these men recently formed the Southern Utah Independent Forest Products Association. For years, small operators had been getting the leavings from big timber sales promoted by the Forest Service in Dixie and Fishlake National Forests and sold to major corporations, Louisiana Pacific chief among them. The small operators had eked out a living mainly by supplying timbers to the coal mining industry. Then the industry switched to "long-wall" mining technology, which required little or no timbering. The market for timbers swiftly declined, and the timber operators, like the ranchers, faced hard times. But after they organized, the association's loggers, encouraged by new Forest Service management policies, which emphasized small and more environmentally sensitive timber sales and the promotion of local economies, got a "revitalization" grant from the agency and hired the Mater Engineering Company in Oregon to undertake a study of marketing opportunities for log cabins, flooring, roundwood furniture, cabinets, specialty fencing, and other "value-added" wood products. "The theory," Williams said, "is that you make more money by cutting fewer trees. And the ultimate goal is to come up with what is a sustainable cut for the forest, something that everyone can agree on."

Such grassroots efforts may or may not keep at least some traditional industries alive in southern Utah, but the region's future almost certainly lies with tourism. And, if tourism's impact on the land is a little less direct than that of the purely extractive industries (over the long haul, of course, too many people in too few places can do significant levels of very real damage, as we have learned in places like Yosemite National Park), its effect on human communities is immediate. Ray Potter has seen (and helped define) what that has meant. On a Sunday afternoon fourteen years ago—just about the time I was hiking though the translucent maples of Water Canyon a couple of hundred miles away—he and his wife, Diane, went to a bluff overlooking the intersection of Highways 24 and 12. Ray, born in nearby Loa into a Mormon ranching and farming family, was then a highway construction engineer for the state and had helped to pave Highway 12. He and Diane had made a decent life for themselves and their five children, but they had larger ambitions. "We sat up here on this hill and we counted the cars," he remembered. "I said, 'Diane, this would be a good place to build a motel.' After that we couldn't talk or think about anything else."

The result was a complex that now includes not only the Wonderland Inn, with its indoor swimming pool, conference center, beauty parlor, restaurant, and fifty rooms in two separate units, but also a service station, convenience store, and RV campground at the bottom of the hill next to Highway 12 and the Torrey cemetery. "I would say that Highway 12 traffic has tripled since we started to build here," Ray said. With traffic has come opportunity, and not just for the Potters. There is another gas station-cum-convenience store across the road from theirs now, and down the road sit two spanking new motels, while on Highway 24 toward Capitol Reef National Park, a big new Holiday Inn has just sprouted.

Thirty-five miles away on Highway 12, over Boulder Mountain, Boulder also is feeling the stretch marks of growth. The town was founded in a beautiful little valley as a Mormon ranching community in 1894, and when I first encountered it more than ten years ago, it seemed to have changed little from the days of its origins. Situated where Highway 12 meets the Burr Trail, the town then boasted two main attractions: Anasazi Indian Village State Park, the site of a prehistoric settlement, and the tiny Burr Trail Cafe, a former gas station

144

not quite the size of a double-wide, where the legendary Billie Jones, the best-looking great-grandmother west of the Mississippi and north of a given point, specialized in meals that would founder a horse at prices that would have delighted Jack Benny. "Feed me!" I used to cry, crawling up on a stool after four or five days of solitary backpacking in the nearby canyons of the Escalante River, living on little more than gorp, river water, and happiness. And feed me she did, mounding the food up and serving it while bantering cheerfully with cowboys, truck drivers, and a few tourists.

The Burr Trail Cafe is no more, though Billie remains in town. But up the road is a motel that wasn't there ten years ago, and right across Highway 12 from Billie's old cafe, a publisher and developer from the urban clot of the Wasatch Front is completing a resort complex that will ultimately feature a trading store, a public bathhouse for local hikers, a small museum, and cabins for the use of writers and artists.

All this is a little unsettling to a pilgrim like me, who once thought of Boulder as a tiny, stable island of rural amenity in a wide sea of wilderness, something you could count on to gently help you decompress after perhaps a little too much solitude. But behind the cafe is something that suggests that even growth is not necessarily a bad thing. This is the Boulder Mountain Lodge, a twenty-room resort and restaurant artfully crafted from local wood and stone and snuggled up against a nine-acre pond sweet with the sound of birdsong. The four-year-old lodge is the work of Mark and Katie Austin, who bought the entire pond in order to keep it preserved as a wetland. They also have purchased 870 acres on the mesa that rises just behind them, Austin tells me as we sit by the pond on a beautiful morning, watching yellow-headed blackbirds, ruddy ducks, swallows, and redheads go about their noisy business among the reeds and waters.

"What do you plan to do with the new property?" I asked him.

"Oh, put in a couple of hundred second homes, a little shopping center, a jetport," he answered with a straight face.

It took me a beat or two to get the joke. "Commercial jets or just private?"

"Just private. You wouldn't want to let things get out of hand."

There will be no jetports. What he is really planning to do, Austin admitted, is put some homes up on the far side of the property but keep 90 percent of the land as open space, about the only way it is ever likely to be preserved. "You have to own it to zone it," he said. The town has virtually no zoning regulations, and those that do exist are indifferently enforced. He is certain that if he and Katie had not bought the land, sooner or later the rim of the mesa would have been alive with condominiums. "I keep a file of people who have come by here and inquired about property in Boulder," he said. "I counted it the day before yesterday and it had 562 names—including operators from Las Vegas. 'This would make a hell of a nice place to put some condos and golf courses,' they say, showing no sensitivity whatever about one of the most beautiful, pristine places left anywhere in the Southwest."

Austin, a transplant and a trench-warfare veteran of the conservation battles of the Reagan years, has managed to combine careers as a well-respected contractor and an outspoken environmental activist. His opinion with regard to wilderness, for example, was summed up in the remark he used to toss out with regard to the Redrock Wilderness Act's old figure of 5.7 million acres. It had to be a typographical error, he would say—"It should be 7.5 million acres." He is not at all reluctant to point out that the Utah Wilderness Coalition's new proposal of 9.1 million acres validates his joke. At the same time, he is a firm believer in intelligent planning and in searching for ways to keep

146

local industries alive without wrecking the land. He was a major force behind the founding of the Southern Utah Independent Forest Products Association and is helping to promote Dell LeFevre's "Boulder Beef" project, when not hammering at Boulder's city council to get serious about planning. "Unless they come up with a plan that says, 'We can have wilderness and we can keep you in business,' it isn't going to work," he says—speaking not just of Boulder now but of southern Utah generally. "That's what I believe—we can have lots of wilderness, and we can keep the cattle ranches and the small loggers in business, at least to a certain extent. But only if you have a plan that works."

Such comments have made him some enemies among the locals. It appears not to bother him much, and his impatience with the town's lackadaisical zoning traditions was echoed by Larry D. Davis, who took the job as the first and so far only manager of Anasazi State Park more than a quarter of a century ago. Davis likes the idea of millions of acres of wilderness just fine and hopes he lives to see it. He is less sanguine that Boulder will be able to retain the essentially rural, untrammeled character that has made it such a good place to live and bring up his children. "I hope so," he told me one morning, his newly refurbished little museum already beginning to fill with tourists, "but there's people with money coming around, and money seems to talk. I would hate to see this place turn into another Moab. What does it take to scare people?"

MOAB SCARES PEOPLE PLENTY. It scares Ray Potter, over in Torrey, who is generally conservative on the question of wilderness but who would find common ground with Mark Austin when it comes to careful planning. "We've lived here and done what we want, how we want, for so many years that we think we can survive and carry that into the future," Ray said. "Most people think, 'Nobody can tell me what to do on my property.' That's the mentality of people around here. We've had zoning meetings and basically they've failed. It's going to be a slow process, a very slow process, but it will come eventually." It has to come, he believes, because if it doesn't his town could become another, albeit smaller, version of Moab.

Poor Moab. It seems to have become a symbol of the region's ambivalence toward growth. In some respects, it has no one to blame but itself, having recently encouraged an end-of-century boom whose most flamboyant characteristics are reminiscent of those that stretched the limits of the little town during the uranium rush of the 1950s—and while both Moab and Grand County have met the consequent problems with perhaps a greater level of civic competence this time around, Moab still bubbles and spurts with an unruly, almost uncontrolled energy.

For a while, in the 1980s, such a state of affairs seemed unlikely. The Atlas Corporation, Moab's largest employer, laid off 175 workers from its labor force of 500 in 1983, and in early 1984, after the price for uranium concentrate dropped from $44 to $18 a pound, the last vestiges of the uranium boom went bust and Atlas mothballed its mines and its Moab mill. Similar, though less drastic declines in the oil industry and in potash mining added to the county's woes. Unemployment rose to an alarming 19 percent, while 20 percent of the county's population moved on to other parts. Property values plummeted and businesses went under.

Desperately, the county and the town launched a major drive in the 1980s to attract tourists to nearby Arches and Canyonlands National Parks and to the Colorado River as a recreational waterway. It succeeded beyond its most fertile dreams, and by the early 1990s Moab had become a recreational bazaar for river rafters, mountain bikers, RV-equipped sightseers, and four-wheel-drive enthusiasts. By the late 1990s, visitation to Arches National Park was averaging nearly 850,000 people a year, while that at Canyonlands had risen to almost 450,000 a year—both figures nearly double what they had been at the end of the 1980s. There were now thirty-three motels in Moab offering a total of 1,381 rooms, with many additional rooms available in sixteen bed-and-breakfast outfits and other forms of lodging. Every one of them was needed during the high season between May and the end of October, when the invasion of tourists swelled the population in and near Moab from about 7,000 to more than 20,000, putting extraordinary pressure on everything from medical facilities to grocery stores.

No recreational sport grew more astonishingly than mountain biking. In the 7,240-acre Sand Flats Recreation Area just west of town, where the BLM had constructed a fourteen-mile loop called the Slickrock Trail around and over towering cream-colored lumps of "petrified dunes," mountain bike use bloated from just 140 rides in 1983 to more than 100,000 by the end of 1993, and Sand Flats had become the mountain-biking capital of the world, while at the same time coming under similarly heavy use by four-wheel-drive aficionados. The BLM struggled diligently to enforce fire, camping, vehicle use, and safety regulations, but it became increasingly helpless in the face of so many people—especially during spring break every year, when Moab took on some of the character and endured some of the hormonal excesses that have made Florida's Fort Lauderdale a name to be reckoned with in the folklore of eastern college campuses and in the bleak language of police reports. In 1993, the comparison became all too appropriate when drunken mountain bikers and four-wheelers came to blows over access to trails and campsites in the Sand Flats, initiating a frenzy of vandalism during which junipers and piñons were ripped up and burned, archeological sites trashed, trails littered with human waste, and motor vehicles driven all over the landscape. The presence of sheriff's deputies was required before what is still remembered as the "Easter Riot" could be brought under control. "We went fishing for a little tourism," Grand County Council member Bill Hedden told researchers for the Sonoran Institute's gateway project, "and hooked a great white shark."

The riot—or the problems it represented—helped inspire the creation, in the fall of that same year, of the Canyon Country Partnership, a body composed of agency officials from the BLM, the National Park Service, and the Forest Service; various state officials; and commissioners from Grand, Carbon, Emery, and San Juan Counties. "The underlying aim of the partnership," the organization's charter declared, "is to maintain the basic health and sustainability of ecosystems, and serve the needs of people depending upon such ecosystems for commodity or non-commodity values." As Hedden, one of its members, described the process, "partners share information and work together to assure that individual decisions make collective sense for the land and the community," and while it has no real power beyond that of persuasion, its first major effort was an apparent success.

The partnership hired Craig Bigler, a professional planner and a resident of Moab, as facilitator, and Bigler worked with Hedden and other county officials to engineer a cooperative management agreement with the BLM that would allow Grand County to set up a fee collection program at the Sand Flats Recreation Area, the money to be used to maintain the area's trails, roads, and campsites, as well as for landscape restoration and education programs to teach users "the right way to be here," as BLM district manager Kate Kitchell put it. A grant from AmeriCorps—the modern, though infinitely more modest, equivalent of the New Deal's Civilian Conservation Corps—enabled the partnership to put together a nine-member Community

Sand Flats Team to do much of the work of maintenance and education under the direction of the BLM, while a Citizens Stewardship Committee would advise the Grand County Commission on how the fee money should be spent. Over the first two years of the program, fees brought in more than $120,000 a year and were expected to average no less than $130,000 a year in the future, and while seasonal vandalism and illegal off-road vehicle use continued, they resulted in much lower levels of damage—and there were no more riots.

Bill Hedden, a former neurobiologist who moved into the area from the East in the 1970s, got a little irritated when I told him that, in spite of high-minded efforts like the Sand Flats agreement, people nevertheless still cite Moab as the kind of place they don't want their towns to become. "I think a lot of those people have never even been here," he said. "What they're really saying is that they're afraid of change. We've seen a tremendous amount of change here, there's no question about it, and change is a mixed bag. Moab has actually got a lot of good things, charming things going on right now." He emphasized such cultural events as the annual summer Arts Festival and the annual fall Music Festival, good restaurants, and some economic diversification, the kind of industrial mix that Grand County is pushing in its promotions ("Grand County is ripe and ready for Light Manufacturers, Community Retail Outlets, Tourist Related Services, High-Tech Industries, Telecommunications, and Film Support Services," reads the blurb on the back of a real estate throwaway).

Still, Hedden is quick to recognize the limits of such arrangements as the Canyon Country Partnership, and while he remains committed to planning as the only logical game in town—he worked hard on the Grand County master plan and describes it as both intelligent and pragmatic—he laments the difficulty of persuading the majority of the town's oldest residents to support anything that limits their ability to do just about anything they want with their property. These are people who are reluctant to admit that it is going to be necessary to cooperate with federal land-managing agencies—especially when they are told they should do so by people such as Hedden, who probably will be considered by many residents to be "outsiders" until the day they die. These traditional people, Hedden said, remain in power because they see themselves locked in a kind of culture war, a fight for survival with newcomers, and when it comes time to vote, they always turn out at the polls to defend what they perceive to be their God-given rights—while the newcomers, less motivated by fear, perhaps, hardly vote at all except during national elections. The result is a kind of social impasse.

"In Moab right now," Hedden said, "we're facing a whole collection of major subdivision requests that are working their way through the planning process, and these traditional people are fighting like crazy to make sure that the developers can get away with anything they want. They just don't get it. Their own policies will eventually result in taxes so high for street construction and maintenance, schools, and other public services that the old-timers won't be able to afford to live here any more. It's like a Greek tragedy."

The town may not be a tragedy, but it certainly is a mess on any given day in May, when it is easy to understand why people in other towns chant Moab's name like an ominous mantra. In the crowded, crawling weekend traffic, dusty old local pickups are outnumbered by out-of-state RVs the size of duplexes, most of them bound for Canyonlands and Arches. Competing with these ungainly monsters for parking spaces and lane access are flocks of four-wheel-drive vehicles. There are new, big-shouldered pickups in whose beds battered-looking dirt bikes have been piled like the wreckage from a terrible accident. Others hold stubby, outsized tricycles called ATVs, tied down like strange-looking animals. Some people strap their dirt bikes to the back end of their vehicles, while others tow everything behind them on trailers. Everywhere, you see cars and vans antlered with mountain-bike parts, wheels and frames outlined against the sky like the skeletal branches of winter trees; over the roofs of others, kayaks and canoes are draped.

Main Street, the funnel through which all this traffic flows, is one extruded strip development that spills through the length of the otherwise lovely valley. It is an architectural phantasmagoria whose motels—some appearing to be under perpetual construction—shopping centers (no malls yet), cutely named restaurants, gift shops, rock shops, art galleries, Indian arts and crafts shops, package stores, gas stations, mountain bike sale and repair shops, river expedition outfitters, and other commercial enterprises stretch the ability of *eclectic* to describe it. "This isn't a community any more," lamented twenty-year resident Jim Stiles, the publisher and editor of the singularly irreverent weekly, the *Canyon Country Zephyr*, "it's a population center."

Hedden wasn't buying that interpretation when I repeated it. "If he means by 'community' someplace small," he responded with a laugh, "well, yeah, Moab's growing, and there are a lot more visitors here. But there are also many subcommunities in the town that are probably a heck of a lot more vibrant than they used to be. If you want human resources, Moab is much richer than it was. It's just more of everything, more of the good things and more of the bad things. If you focus just on what the place used to be when life was simpler and quieter, there's not really any reply to that, but there's a lot of excitement and hope in what is going on right now."

So, with economic and demographic changes coming faster than they can be tracked, with the fate of more than nine million acres of wilderness all around them still unsettled, with environmentalists, antienvironmentalists, and city, county, state, and federal officials squabbling among one another over decisions that will shape their lives for good or ill, the citizens of southern Utah try to puzzle out their future with a mixture of anxiety, anger, wonder, and hope. And maybe something else, too. "There's a certain pride about this country that Utahns have," Ed Lueders, the poet-pianist of Torrey, mused to me during one of our talks, "people who have been here a hell of a lot longer than I have." I don't think he meant the kind of mindless braggadocio that gets expressed in handouts and advertisements from the Utah Travel Council or on postcards, T-shirts, and calendars. The pride of which he spoke goes deeper, down to where people live, where they think, where they dream; it can also be called love. I found it everywhere I went, in just about everyone to whom I talked, including those who said they hated the idea of wilderness and among those who might otherwise appear to lack a single philosophical bone in their bodies. Billie Jones had such love; so did Dell LeFevre and Bill Hedden and Mark Austin and Larry Davis.

And so did Ray Potter, the commonsensical descendant of Mormon pioneers. I remember encountering him as I came out of my room at the Wonderland Inn one October morning during my last trip. The day was cool but clear and the wind had not yet started whipping through the flats, carrying the gelid hint of the winter to come. The sun was rising from one horizon while above the other a ghostly, crescent-shaped sliver of moon was just barely visible in the pale blue of the sky. Ray was leaning against the side of the building with a cup of coffee in his hand, looking up at the big wall of Boulder Mountain, its gunmetal blue shoulders streaked here and there with golden patches of aspen leaves turning with the season. I joined him, and after exchanging greetings, we didn't say much, just stood there on this good morning, holding up the building while the sun warmed our faces and began painting the mountain with the delicate brush of light. He was still there when I left, and I didn't need to ask him why.

The mountain was speaking to Ray Potter, I think, helping him to pin down and define his own human place in the heart-stopping spread of landscape all around him; no matter what he may have felt about the pragmatism of planning or the need to institutionalize wilderness through legislation, what he was demonstrating in his moment of silent tribute that morning was a species of love as profound as it was mute.

Love is a powerful tool, and maybe, just maybe, before the last little town is corrupted and the last of the unroaded and undeveloped wildness is given over to dreams of profit, maybe it *will* be love, finally, love for the land for its own sake and for what it holds of beauty and joy and spiritual redemption, that will make the redrock country of southern Utah not a battlefield but a revelation.

MAPS OF UTAH

GOOD TRAVELLERS—even armchair travelers—use good maps. Fine maps are very useful in the canyon country of wild Utah, especially the 1:250,000-scale topographic quadrangles of the U.S. Geological Survey.

For this book, two general maps are provided to assist in reading and general orientation: one of wild Utah and one showing the major gateway airports to the region. They should be supplemented by other maps when exploring Utah in the field.

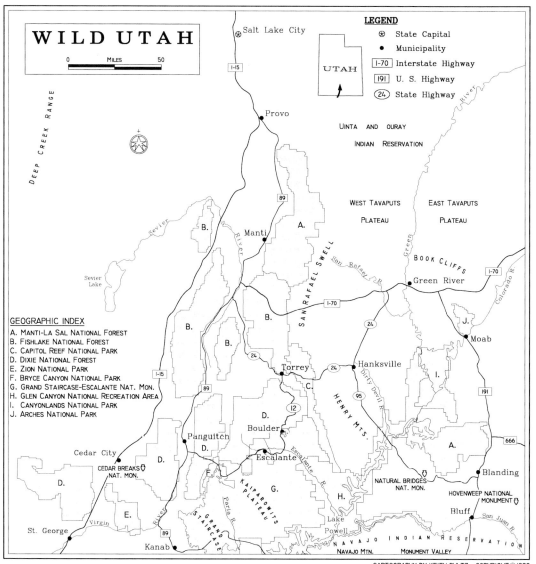

WILD UTAH

0 MILES 50

LEGEND
⊗ State Capital
• Municipality
I-70 Interstate Highway
191 U. S. Highway
24 State Highway

UTAH

Salt Lake City
I-15
Provo
89
Manti

UINTA AND OURAY
INDIAN RESERVATION

WEST TAVAPUTS   EAST TAVAPUTS
PLATEAU   PLATEAU

DEEP CREEK RANGE

Sevier River

Sevier Lake

San Rafael R.

Green River

BOOK CLIFFS
I-70
Green River
Colorado R.

SAN RAFAEL SWELL
I-70

J.
Moab

24
Hanksville
I.

GEOGRAPHIC INDEX
A. MANTI-LA SAL NATIONAL FOREST
B. FISHLAKE NATIONAL FOREST
C. CAPITOL REEF NATIONAL PARK
D. DIXIE NATIONAL FOREST
E. ZION NATIONAL PARK
F. BRYCE CANYON NATIONAL PARK
G. GRAND STAIRCASE-ESCALANTE NAT. MON.
H. GLEN CANYON NATIONAL RECREATION AREA
I. CANYONLANDS NATIONAL PARK
J. ARCHES NATIONAL PARK

B.
B.
B.
24
Torrey
C.
24
95
Dirty Devil R.
HENRY MTS.
191

I-15
89
D.
12
Boulder
D.
Panguitch
D.
Cedar City
CEDAR BREAKS
NAT. MON.
Escalante
F.
G.
Escalante R.
NATURAL BRIDGES
NAT. MON.
A.
666
Blanding
HOVENWEEP NATIONAL
MONUMENT

D.
D.
E.
St. George
Virgin
River
Parla R.
KAIPAROWITS PLATEAU
GRAND STAIRCASE
Kanab
89
H.
Lake Powell
Bluff
San Juan R.

NAVAJO INDIAN RESERVATION
NAVAJO MTN.   MONUMENT VALLEY

AIRPORT CONNECTIONS TO SOUTHERN UTAH

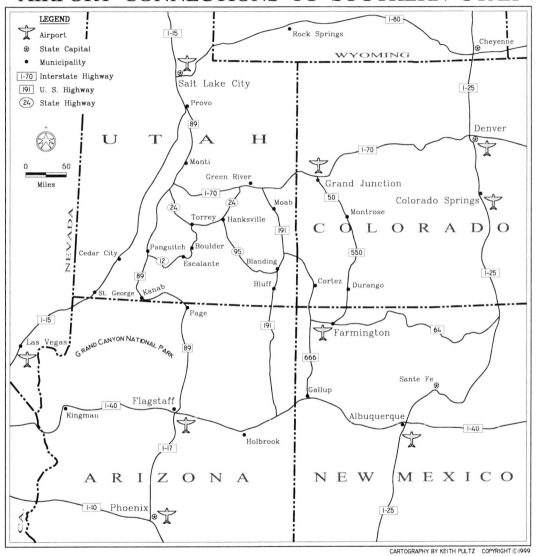

SUGGESTED READINGS

Abbey, Edward. *Desert Solitaire: A Season in the Wilderness*. New York: Ballantine Books, 1968.

———. *The Journey Home: Some Words in Defense of the American West*. New York: E. P. Dutton, 1977.

Barnes, F. A. *Canyon Country Geology for the Layman and Rockhound*. Salt Lake City: Wasatch Publishers, 1978.

Barrs, Donald L. *The Colorado Plateau: A Geologic History*. Albuquerque: University of New Mexico Press, 1983.

Bowers, Janice Emily. *Shrubs and Trees of the Southwestern Deserts*. Tucson: Southwest Parks and Monuments Association, 1993.

Bruhn, Arthur F. Revised and updated by Nicky Leach. *Exploring Southern Utah's Land of Color*. Springdale, Utah: Zion Natural History Association, 1993.

Chronic, Halka. *Pages of Stone: Geology of Western National Parks and Monuments*. Vol 4. *Grand Canyon and the Plateau Country*. Seattle: Mountaineers, 1988.

Cole, Sally. *Legacy on Stone: Rock Art of the Colorado Plateau and Four Corners Region*. Boulder, Colo.: Johnson Books, 1990.

Cordell, Linda S. *Prehistory of the Southwest.* New York: Academic Press, 1984.

Federal Writers' Project. *Utah: A Guide to the State.* New York: Hastings House, 1941.

Firmage, Richard A. *A History of Grand County.* Grand County: Utah State Historical Society, 1996.

Fontana, Bernard L. *Entrada: The Legacy of Spain and Mexico in the United States.* Tucson: Southwest Parks and Monuments Association, 1994.

Harper, Kimball T., et al., eds. *Natural History of the Colorado Plateau and the Great Basin.* Niwot: University Press of Colorado, 1994.

Inskip, Eleanor, ed. *The Colorado River through Glen Canyon before Lake Powell. History Photo Journal, 1872 to 1964.* Moab, Utah: Inskip, 1995.

Mails, Thomas E., and Dan Evehema. *Hotevilla: Hopi Shrine of the Covenant.* New York: Marlowe and Co., in association with Touch the Earth Foundation, 1996.

Martin, Russell. *A Story That Stands Like a Dam: Glen Canyon and the Struggle for the Soul of the West.* New York: Henry Holt, 1989.

Mather, Cotton, P. P. Karen, and George F. Thompson. *Beyond the Great Divide: Denver to the Grand Canyon.* New Brunswick, N.J.: Rutgers University Press, 1992.

McPherson, Robert S. *A History of San Juan County: In the Palm of Time.* San Juan County: Utah State Historical Society and the San Juan County Commission, 1995.

Meyer, Larry L. "The Time of the Great Fever." *American Heritage,* June/July 1981.

Ringholz, Raye C. *Uranium Frenzy: Boom and Bust on the Colorado Plateau.* New York: W. W. Norton, 1989.

Roberts, David. *In Search of the Old Ones: Exploring the Anasazi World of the Southwest.* New York: Simon and Schuster, 1996.

Rusho, W. L. *Everett Ruess: A Vagabond for Beauty.* Salt Lake City: Peregrine Smith Books, 1983.

SUGGESTED READINGS

Saner, Reg. *The Four-Legged Falcon: Essays on the Interior West and the Natural Scene*. Baltimore: Johns Hopkins University Press, 1993.

Stegner, Wallace. *Beyond the Hundredth Meridian: John Wesley Powell and the Second Opening of the West*. Boston: Houghton Mifflin, 1954.

_____. *Mormon Country*. New York: Duell, Sloan & Pearce, 1942.

_____. *The Uneasy Chair: A Biography of Bernard DeVoto*. Garden City, N.Y.: Doubleday, 1974.

_____, ed. *The Letters of Bernard DeVoto*. Garden City, N.Y.: Doubleday, 1975.

Strutin, Michele, and George H. H. Huey. *Chaco: A Cultural Legacy*. Tucson: Southwest Parks and Monuments Association, 1994.

Trimble, Stephen, and Terry Tempest Williams, eds. *Testimony: Writers of the West Speak on Behalf of Utah Wilderness*. Minneapolis: Milkweed Editions, 1996.

Utah Wilderness Coalition. *Wilderness at the Edge: A Citizen Proposal to Protect Utah's Canyons and Deserts*. Salt Lake City: Utah Wilderness Coalition, 1990.

Van Cott, John W. *Utah Place Names: A Comprehensive Guide to the Origins of Geographic Names*. Salt Lake City: University of Utah Press, 1990.

Waters, Frank. *The Colorado*. New York: Rinehart, 1946.

Watkins, T. H. *Stone Time: Southern Utah, a Portrait and a Meditation*. Santa Fe: Clear Light Publishers, 1994.

Watkins, T. H., and Charles S. Watson, Jr. *The Lands No One Knows: America and the Public Domain*. San Francisco: Sierra Club, 1975.

Watkins, T. H., et al. *The Grand Colorado: The Story of a River and Its Canyons*. Palo Alto, Calif.: American West Publishing Co., 1969.

Wright, John B. *Rocky Mountain Divide: Selling and Saving the West*. Austin: University of Texas Press, 1994.

Zaslowsky, Dyan, and T. H. Watkins. *These American Lands: Parks, Wilderness, and the Public Lands*. Rev. ed. Washington, D.C.: Island Press, 1994.

ABOUT THE AUTHOR

T. H. Watkins, Wallace Stegner Distinguished Professor of Western American Studies at Montana State University, was the editor of *Wilderness*, the quarterly magazine of the Wilderness Society, for fourteen years. He served as both managing editor, then editor of the *American West* magazine, was an editorial consultant to the Sierra Club, and was a senior editor at *American Heritage* magazine. He is now a contributing editor for *Audubon* magazine. He has written more than three hundred articles and book reviews for some fifty journals, magazines, and newspapers, and is the author, coauthor, or editor of twenty-seven other books on American history, Western American history, and the environment. His 1990 biography of FDR's interior secretary, *Righteous Pilgrim: The Life and Times of Harold L. Ickes, 1874-1952*, won the *Los Angeles Times* Book Award for biography in 1991 and was a finalist for both the National Book Award and the National Book Critics Circle Award. His most recent books are *Natural America* (1998) and *The Hungry Years: A Narrative History of the Great Depression in America* (1999).

LIBRARY OF CONGRESS CATALOGING-IN-PUBLICATION DATA

Watkins, T. H. (Tom H.). 1936–
      The Redrock chronicles : saving wild Utah / T.H. Watkins ; with
photographs by the author. — 1st ed.
            p.   cm. — (Center books on space, place, and time)
      ISBN 0-8018-6237-X. — ISBN 0-8018-6238-8 (pbk. : alk. paper)
      1. Landscape protection—Utah.   2. Natural history—Utah.
3. Utah—History.   I. Center for American Places (Harrisonburg,
Va.)   II. Title.   III. Series.
QH76.5.U8W28   2000
508.792′5—dc21   99-27001
                                                                          CIP